Simple & Stylish
Bead Accents

Katie Hacker

©2005 Katie Hacker
Published by

 **kp books**
An imprint of F+W Publications, Inc.

700 East State Street • Iola, WI 54990-0001
715-445-2214 • 888-457-2873

Our toll-free number to place an order or obtain a free catalog is 800-258-0929.

Library of Congress Catalog Number: 2004098428

ISBN: 0-87349-924-7

Edited by Candy Wiza
Designed by Emily Adler

Printed in the United States of America

Dedication

This book is dedicated to the people who have seen my projects in magazines or books and have contacted me with questions or comments. Thank you for your enthusiasm and generosity of spirit! Your suggestions have given me much-needed direction and inspiration.

Acknowledgments

I would like to thank my husband, Craig, for his unflagging understanding and support in our life together, especially while I was writing this book. I give thanks every day that we met and recognized a soul mate in each other. From giving me pep talks to being in charge of meals, he was instrumental in making this book happen.

I also am grateful to have a wonderful and supportive family. My parents, Jerry and Dee Hacker, and my sister, Laura, are the kind of family that any person would be lucky to have. This book is a better resource because of their contributions. Special thanks go to my mom for sharing her editorial skills. I'm also thankful to my second family, the Browns, for all of the everyday ways that they contributed to this book's completion, including Connie's sewing guidance and assistance.

Boundless thanks to the companies who provided materials for use in this book and to the other professionals who gave me advice and direction.

Special thanks to my editor, Candy Wiza, for sharing her friendship and talent; photographer Robert Best; designer Emily Adler; and acquisitions editor Julie Stephani for lending their expertise.

Introduction

There's something magical about beads. The variety of colors, shapes and sizes alone is amazing. The projects in this book feature jewelry-inspired techniques for incorporating beading into a variety of fun projects for gifts, home decor and fashion.

My love for beading began in junior high, before I had pierced ears. After many frustrating searches for cool clip earrings, I decided to learn how to make my own. I've been designing beaded jewelry ever since. And you've probably heard it before, but beading can be addictive! Now I want to put beads on everything. And that's where I got the idea for this book.

Adding beads to a finished surface, whether it's a gift box, a candleholder or a denim jacket, gives that piece a personality and sparkle that makes it uniquely yours. Substitute beads or change colors to suit your own taste.

Learn my tips and tricks for creating easy beaded designs, and then use the projects in this book as springboards for your own imagination.

Table of Contents

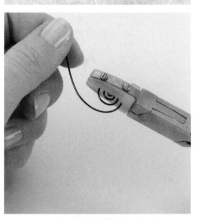

Chapter 4: Home Decor 70

Chapter 5: Fashion 102

Resource Guide 128

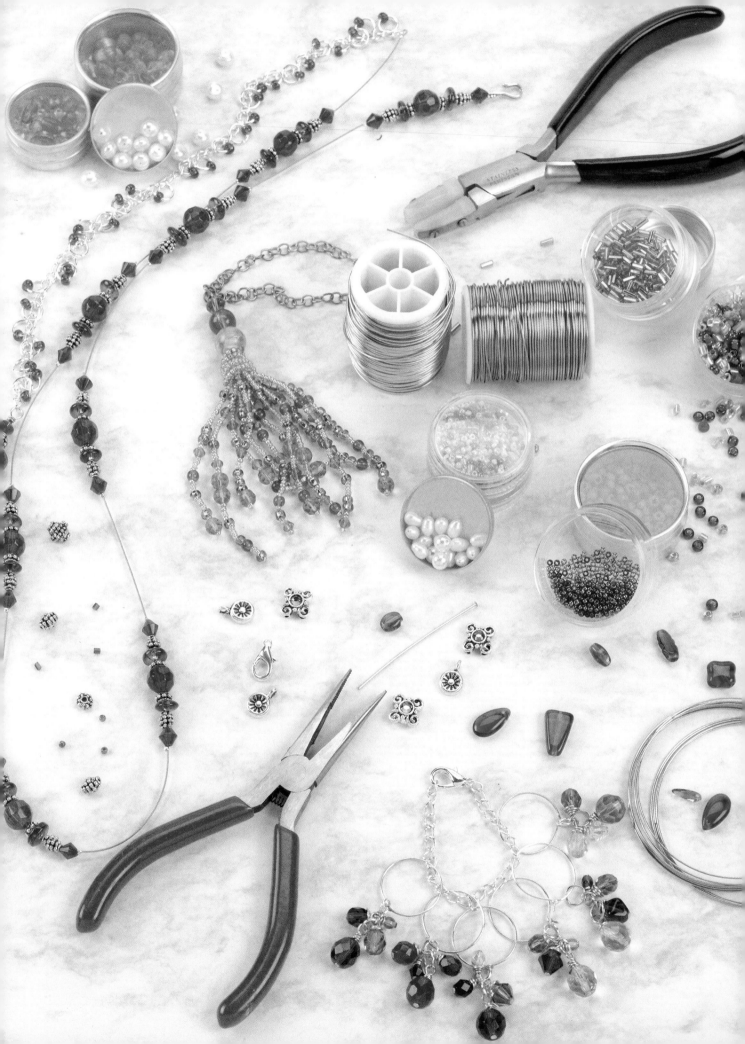

Chapter 1: Supplies

In this chapter, you'll learn about a variety of supplies that make beading easier. Beads, tools, adhesives and other supplies that are used in this book are identified and explained. There's even a section on organizers. Let's get started!

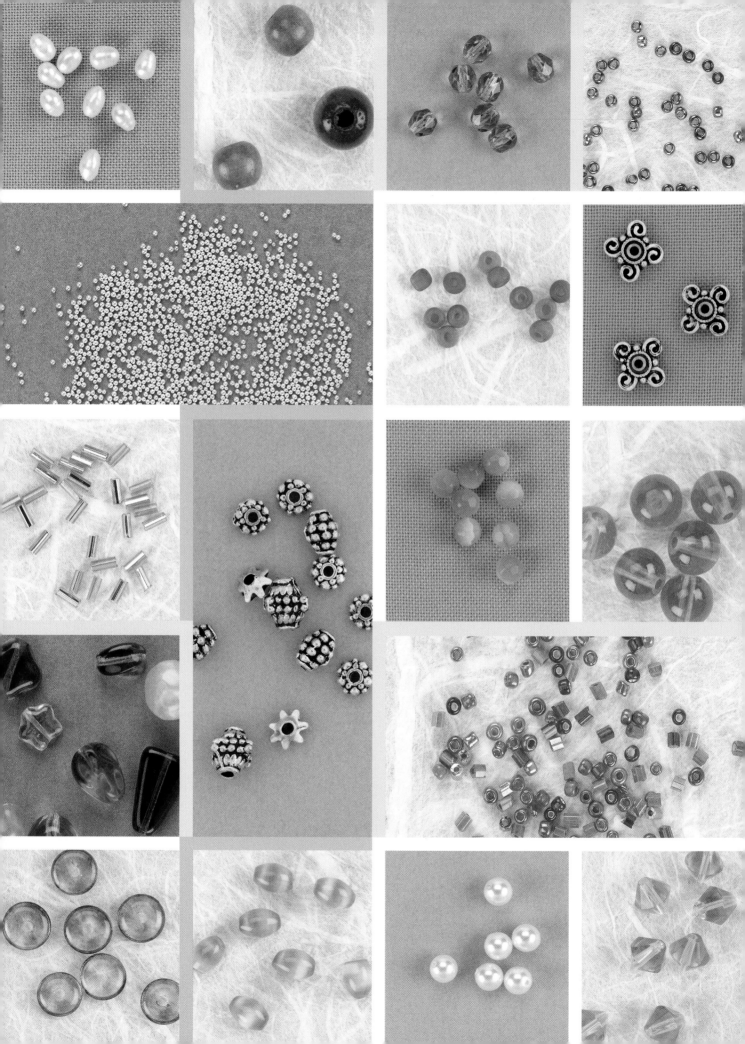

Beads

Anything with a hole in it can be used as a bead. In fact, the earliest beads were made from natural materials such as shells, stones, animal bones and teeth. Today, beads still are made from those materials, in addition to a variety of others. They are available in a myriad of colors, styles, shapes and sizes. Every culture has used beads in some way, which makes beading one of the most ancient, cross-cultural art forms.

1 Seed Beads

Named for their resemblance to seeds, seed beads are typically sold by size. The smaller the number, the larger the size; hence size 6/0 beads (also called "E" beads) are larger than size 11/0 beads. Seed bead mixes usually are inexpensive and include a variety of sizes, shapes and colors.

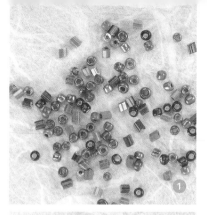

2 Bugle Beads

Bugle beads are long, cylindrical beads that are small in diameter, like seed beads. Twisted bugles are particularly sparkly.

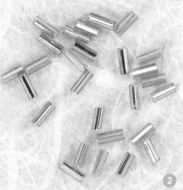

3 Firepolish Beads

These beads are shaped in a mold and flame-polished to remove any imperfections. The result is a shiny finish with slightly rounded, faceted-looking edges.

4 Bicone Beads

A bicone has two tapered ends and is wider in the center, as if two cones were placed together at the widest part. Sometimes the cones are faceted to create extra sparkle.

5 Rondelles

This is a generic term for a flat, disk-shaped bead. They're made from a variety of materials and are often used as spacers.

6 Wooden Beads

For macramé projects, look for wooden beads with large holes. They come in a wide variety of shapes, sizes and colors.

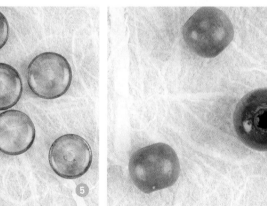

7 Round Glass Beads

Available in a variety of shapes and colors, round glass beads are typically made in molds. High quality beads are perfectly uniform.

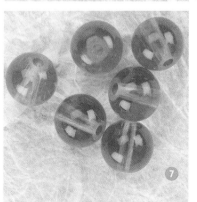

⑧ Cat's Eye Beads

Made from a special blend of glass and fiber optic material, cat's eye beads have a reflective band across the center. The reflective band catches the light and creates an illusion of movement on the bead.

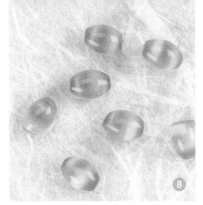

⑨ Freshwater and Glass Pearls

Freshwater pearls are harvested from mussels that inhabit freshwater lakes and rivers. Because they're widely available and are typically abnormally shaped, they are much more economical than cultured pearls. Glass pearls are made by adding a lustrous, pearlescent finish to smooth, round glass beads.

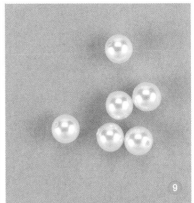

⑩ Metal Spacers

There are many styles of metal spacer beads. Some of the projects in this book include round, square or diamond-shaped spacers.

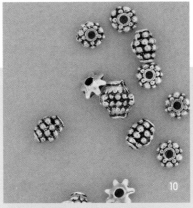

⑪ Metal Slides

Slides have two holes on each end of the bead. They're great for double-strand designs because they separate the strands and add a decorative touch.

⑫ Assorted Glass Beads

Pressed glass beads come in a variety of shapes and colors. They're traditionally made in the Czech Republic.

⑬ Beaded Trim

Store-bought beaded trim is available in a wide variety of colors and styles. You can also make your own customized beaded trim (see page 27).

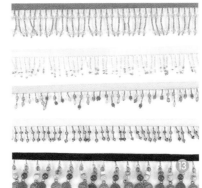

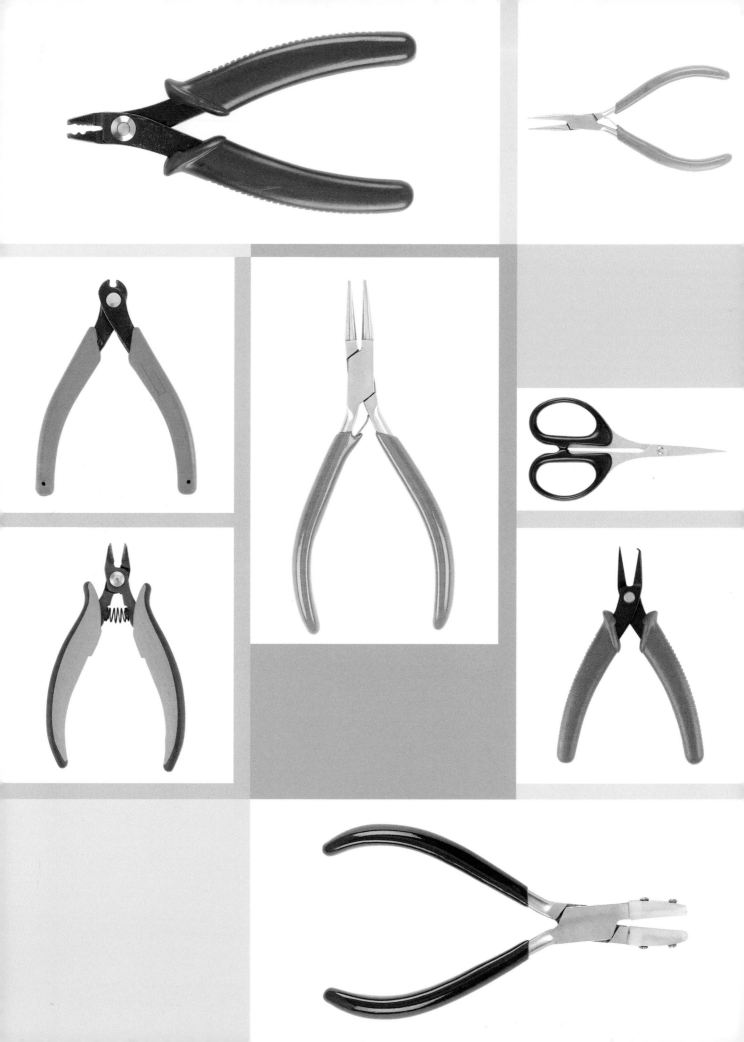

Beading Tools

Only a few basic tools are needed for most beading projects. The four I use most are round nose pliers, chain nose pliers, wire cutters and a crimping tool. Specialty tools that are used for some of the projects in this book include beading scissors, memory wire shears, split ring pliers and nylon jaw pliers.

① Round Nose Pliers

These pliers have tapered round jaws that are useful for making loops and curves. For smooth loops, place the tips of the pliers on the wire, and then turn the pliers.

② Chain Nose Pliers

A jewelry maker's version of needle nose pliers, chain nose pliers have tapered half-round jaws that are smooth inside. Use them to bend wire at right angles and for opening and closing jump rings or wire loops.

③ Wire Cutters

For beading, use a side cutter with small tips to ensure a smooth, close cut. Do not use these to cut memory wire, because it will damage the blades.

④ Crimping Tool

Use this tool with crimp tubes or beads for a secure, professional-looking finish.

⑤ Beading Scissors

Choose scissors with very sharp blades and small tips for cutting in tight places.

❻ Beading Needles

There are many different kinds of beading needles. The main difference between beading needles and sewing needles is that beading needles are not tapered. Use hard beading needles (or very small sewing needles) for sewing beads onto fabric. Use collapsible eye or big eye needles for bead stringing and weaving.

❼ Needle Threader

These mostly are used with hard beading needles. Place the pointed end through the needle eye, place the thread in it, and then pull it back through the eye. If you don't have a needle threader, remember that it is always easier to hold the thread end still in one hand and use the other hand to press the needle eye down onto it.

❽ Memory Wire Shears

These shears are specially designed for cutting hard wire, which will damage ordinary wire cutters.

❾ Split Ring Pliers

Designed specifically for opening and closing split rings, these pliers make it quick and easy to attach rings.

❿ Nylon Jaw Pliers

Use these special pliers when wire wrapping to prevent the pliers from marring the surface of the wire.

Stringing Materials

There are many different kinds of bead stringing materials available today. The projects in this book will teach you a lot of creative ways to use them in gift, home decor and fashion projects.

❶ Flexible Beading Wire

Soft and strong, beading wire is a nylon-coated wire that is made from stranded threads of miniature stainless steel wire. The number of miniature wires determines its flexibility: 49-strand is more flexible than 7-strand. Choose the diameter and number of strands based on the bead hole size, weight of the project and desired drape. Use crimp beads and tubes with beading wire.

❷ Stretchy Cord

Single-strand stretchy cord is available in a variety of colors and diameters. It's commonly used for simple stretchy bracelets. Tie the ends and secure them with a drop of jeweler's cement.

❸ Stretchy Thread

Multiple-strand stretchy thread usually is white and is available in a variety of diameters. It is softer and more flexible than stretchy cord. Use it for bead weaving and stitching.

❹ Memory Wire

Memory wire is tempered wire that "remembers" its shape. It is available in necklace, bracelet and ring size. Only use shears that are specially made to cut hardened wire, because memory wire will ruin ordinary wire cutters.

❺ Craft Wire

The wire used in this book is tarnish-resistant, enamel-coated copper wire. It is available in a wide variety of colors and is fairly inexpensive. The smaller the number, the larger the diameter: 16-gauge wire is larger than 26-gauge wire.

❻ Beading Thread

Beading thread is a strong, braided thread that is available in a range of diameters. Look for thread that is specially designed to provide strength with very little or no stretch. Use the largest diameter possible for the bead hole size.

❼ Hemp Cord

This natural-fiber cord commonly is used for macramé projects. Natural-colored cord in 20 lb. test weight is the most common and widely available style.

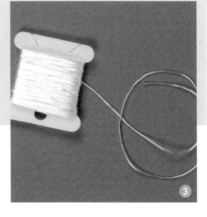

Findings

"Findings" is a general term that refers to the various clasps, head pins, jump rings and other small parts that are used in beading. They typically are made from metal, but can also be made from glass, polymer clay or other materials. The following findings are used in this book.

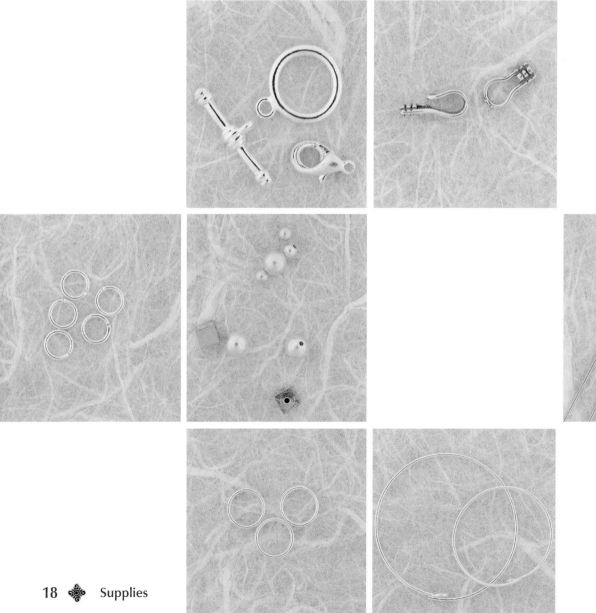

① Head Pins

Head pins are thin wires with flattened ends. They resemble very thin nails and are used to make beaded charms and dangles. Some head pins have decorative embellishments on the end instead of a nail head. They are available in various lengths.

② Eye Pins

Eye pins are similar to head pins except they have a loop, or "eye," on one end. They also are used to make beaded charms and bead links.

③ Jump Rings

Jump rings are made from wire and are sized by diameter. Use them to attach charms and clasps to beaded designs. Open the ends at a 90-degree angle instead of pulling them directly away from each other.

④ Split Rings

Basically a doubled jump ring, split rings are used when a more secure connection is needed. They look like miniature key rings and are opened the same way. Use them to create extension chains or to add clasps to heavy designs.

⑤ Crimp Beads and Tubes

Use crimp beads and tubes instead of knots when working with flexible beading wire for a secure, professional-looking finish. Do not use crimp beads with thread because they can cut through the fibers.

⑥ Crimp Clasp

A crimp clasp is a special clasp that works similarly to a crimp tube. To attach it to a beading wire, place the wire inside the crimp. Use the outer jaws of a crimping tool to squeeze the sides together.

⑦ Clasps

Clasps are used to attach the ends of a beaded design together. There are many different styles. Popular clasps include the toggle and lobster styles.

⑧ Bead Caps

A bead cap is a metal or glass bead that is concave on one side. String the concave part next to a bead so that it "caps" the bead. Use bead caps to add interest to a beaded design.

⑨ End Caps

End caps are available in a variety of shapes and sizes. They are drilled on one side and can be glued onto the ends of memory wire or eye pins.

⑩ Beading Hoops

A beading hoop is a wire hoop with a loop on one end. String beads onto the hoop, then use chain nose pliers to make a 90-degree angle on one end. Place this bent end through the loop to fasten the hoop. Beading hoops are typically used for wine charms or other decorative accents.

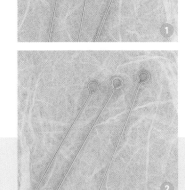

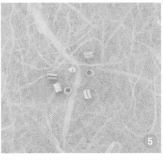

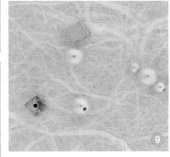

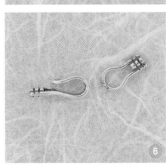

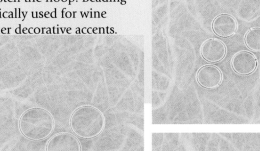

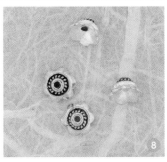

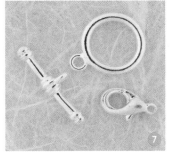

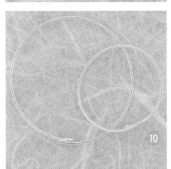

Adhesives

A wide variety of adhesives are used in this book, from standard craft glue and double-sided adhesive, to specialized jeweler's glues. Follow the instructions on the package for their safe and successful use.

❶ Craft Glue

Nontoxic and water-based, this white glue provides a reliable bond for porous surfaces, such as wood and leather. I prefer to use a high-performance version that also works as contact cement for nonporous surfaces.

❷ Glue for Glass and Metal

I typically rely on heavy-duty glues to attach nonporous surfaces, like glass and metal. They are generally quick-drying and provide a strong bond.

❸ Decoupage Gel

Many different kinds of decoupage gels are available. My favorite is a lightweight gel that also can be used as a sealer.

❹ Dimensional Glaze

I use dimensional glaze to seal projects that are covered with seed beads and marbles. You can use any kind of thick, water-based sealer.

❺ Jeweler's Cement

This glue provides a strong, flexible bond for jewelry and beading applications. The tube typically has a very fine tip for precision applications, which makes it perfect for gluing small parts together.

❻ Cyanoacrylic Glue

Quick-drying, permanent bonds are the trademarks of this common "super" glue.

❼ Fabric Glue

The best fabric glues are permanent, quick-drying and washable.

❽ Double-Sided Adhesive

Available in strips, dots, sheets and tape, double-sided adhesive is a quick, clean method for attaching two surfaces together. It is particularly useful for cards and scrapbook pages, but also can be used to attach seed beads and tiny marbles to a surface. You can use the ordinary office supply variety of double-sided tape for paper projects, but use extra sticky glue dots or strips for adhering three-dimensional or other more substantial objects.

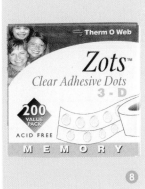

Organizers

Keeping your beads, tools and other supplies organized is the key to making last-minute gifts even easier. If possible, claim a space of your own that is just for craft projects. Organize your beads in divided containers by color or style, and use plastic shoeboxes to store larger craft supplies. Label the outside of each container so you can find things quickly.

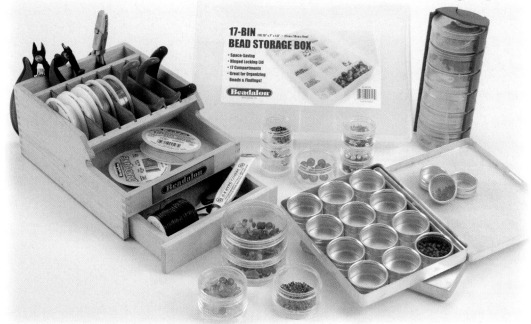

① Bead Mat

This indispensable little piece of fabric creates an instant work surface and prevents beads from rolling away while you're beading, which helps keep things organized.

② Divided Storage Boxes

I like to keep beads in these divided bins because they're easy to store. I separate beads by color family (orange/brown) or style (pearls) and stack them on plastic file trays. When traveling, place a bead mat inside of the lid to keep beads from falling out of their compartments.

③ Stackable Containers

These screw-on containers make it easy to separate beads by color and style. They're available in different sizes and can be stored on your work surface, in a drawer or in plastic shoeboxes.

④ Wooden Organizer

A wooden organizer provides handsome desktop storage for pliers, spools, beads, findings and more. This would prevent my typical pre-project search for tools, if I could remember to always put them back in the proper places.

⑤ Tin Containers

These portable tins make it easy to take your beading projects with you. Take them to class or on the road.

Other Household Items

You also can use other household items to store and organize beads. Experiment with a thread rack, tackle box, spice rack or plastic shoebox to see which ones work best for your bead collection.

Chapter 2: Techniques

A few basic techniques are all it takes to make beaded accents. Learn how to open a jump ring, use a crimping tool and more. You'll be beading in no time!

Opening and Closing a Jump Ring

Use chain nose pliers to turn one side of a jump ring sideways instead of pulling the ends directly away from each other.

Closed jump ring

Open jump ring

Using a Crimping Tool

❶ Place a crimp bead or tube in the inner jaws of the crimping tool. Squeeze hard to create an indentation.

❷ Remove the crimp and turn it 90 degrees. Place it in the outer jaws of the tool and squeeze gently to fold it in half.

❸ To use a crimp bead to attach a clasp: Thread the crimp bead onto the wire; place the wire end through the clasp and back inside the crimp bead to form a loop. Crimp it.

❶ *Crimp in inner jaw*

❷ *Crimp in outer jaw*

❸ *Crimp attaching clasp*

Making a Beaded Charm

❶ String beads onto a head pin or eye pin. Use chain nose pliers to bend the wire in a 90-degree angle above the top bead.

❷ Place round nose pliers ⅛" to ¼" away from the angle and roll them back toward the wire stem to form a loop.

❸ To make a simple loop, cut off any extra wire. To make a wrapped loop, use chain nose pliers to hold the loop, then use your fingers to wrap the extra wire around the stem. Wrapped loops are more secure than simple loops.

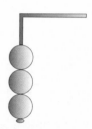

❶ *Beaded Charm*

❷ *Simple loop*

❸ *Wrapped loop*

Tying an Overhand Knot

Wrap the strand (or strands) in a loop, and place the end through the loop.

Overhand Knot

Tying a Half Knot

A half knot is the knot that you use to tie your shoe. Wrap one strand over and under the other strand.

Half Knot

Tying a Square Knot

A square knot is made of two half knots tied in opposite directions.

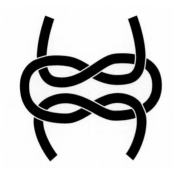

Square Knot

Making Beaded Trim

I recommend purchasing beaded trim because it is widely available in a variety of colors and styles. However, if you want to make your own, follow these instructions: Purchase 3/8" wide ribbon and coordinating beads. Thread a needle, and knot the end. Stitch through the ribbon near the edge. String beads onto the thread, ending with a seed bead. Stitch back through all of the beads except for the last one. Stitch through the ribbon, and tie a knot. Leave 1/4" to 3/8" space on the ribbon, and make another beaded fringe.

Beaded Trim

Making a Wire Coil

Wrap a piece of wire tightly around a dowel to create a nice, even coil. For a more random look, make looser wraps.

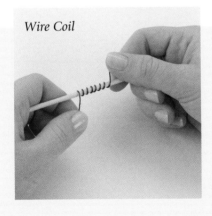

Wire Coil

Backstitching Through a Bead

To backstitch through a bead, string a bead onto the thread. Stitch through the fabric and through the bead again. Use this technique to attach one bead on an embroidered chain of beads.

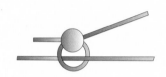

Backstitch

Making a Beaded Branch

String a bead onto the center of a piece of wire. Double the wire, then twist it together.

Beaded Branch

Making a Beaded Daisy

String small beads onto wire or thread. Place the end through the first bead to form a circle. String a larger bead onto the wire or thread, and then place the end back through the third or fourth small bead.

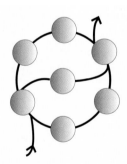

Beaded Daisy

Making a Wire Spiral

❶ Use round nose pliers to make a loop on one end of a piece of wire.

❷ Hold the loop between your thumb and forefinger (or use nylon jaw pliers), and turn your wrist to shape the wire into a spiral.

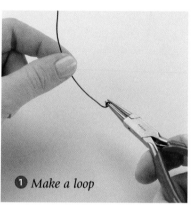

❶ *Make a loop*

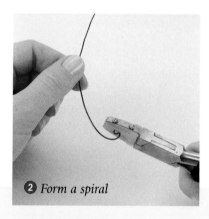

❷ *Form a spiral*

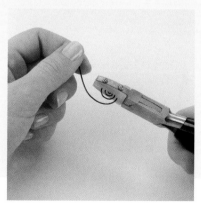

Preparing Unfinished Wooden Items

1 Sand the wooden surface.

2 Use a foam paintbrush to seal the wood with a wood sealant. Sand again lightly if necessary.

3 Paint the wood.

Attaching Seed Beads and Marbles to a Surface

1 Place the object on a paper plate or scrap paper that can be used to collect extra beads. Apply craft glue or double-sided adhesive to the surface.

2 Sprinkle the largest beads over the object.

3 Sprinkle tiny marbles over the object. Add glitter if desired.

4 I like to seal the beads with dimensional glaze to create a truly long-lasting finish.

Craig and I spent two days in Paris during our
European travels. One of my favorite parts of our
visit was riding a giant ferris wheel at sunset. We
also saw the Arc de Triomphe and the Eiffel Tower
and visited the Louvre.

Chapter 3: Gifts

Gifts are a great excuse to bead. In this chapter, you'll learn how to make beaded gifts that look like they're straight from a stylish boutique. You might even be tempted to keep some of them for yourself!

Daisy Gift Box

Materials

4³⁄₈" round ivory papier
  maché box with lid

4¼" silk magenta gerbera daisy

14" multicolored
  (magenta/pink/blue) beaded trim

14½" pink ⁵⁄₈" ribbon

¼" double-sided adhesive tape

Glue for glass and metal

Tools

Wire cutters

Scissors

Pencil

I keep a stash of boxes in different shapes and sizes on hand for last-minute gifts. Use a covered box, a silk flower, store-bought beaded trim and ribbon to embellish packages quickly. It's a pretty little touch that makes your gift even more special.

Instructions

① Apply Adhesive Tape
Place a piece of double-sided adhesive tape on the outside of the lid rim.

② Attach Ribbon to the Lid
Press the wrong side of the ribbon onto the tape. Overlap the ends, and place a small piece of tape on the back of the ribbon end.

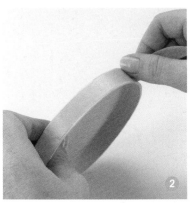

③ Trace the Edge of the Lid
Place the lid on the box. Use a pencil to trace around the lid.

④ Glue a Daisy to the Lid
Remove the daisy from the stem, using wire cutters if necessary. Make the back of the flower as flat as possible. Place a dime-sized drop of glue over the stem hole on the back of the daisy. Glue the daisy to the center of the top of the lid. Add extra glue beneath the bottom petals to hold daisy flat, if necessary.

⑤ Add the Beaded Trim
Remove the lid. Place a piece of double-sided tape around the box below the pencil line. Press the wrong side of the beaded trim onto the tape. Overlap the ends and place a small piece of tape on the back of the trim end.

Tip
Variations:
- *Use several smaller flower heads to cover the top of the lid.*
- *Cover the lid with mixed seed beads and acrylic gems.*
- *Add several layers of beaded trim for added pizzazz.*
- *Cover a gift box with themed scrapbooking paper that hints at what's inside.*

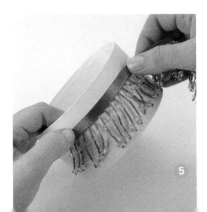

Bead and Ribbon Scrapbook Cover

Materials

12" x 12" linen-covered scrapbook

Ivory photo mat with 3" x 5" opening

14" sheer pink 2⅜" ribbon
  with pastel flowers

4½" x 14½" denim fabric

12¼" square heavyweight white
  paper to fit inside scrapbook cover

4 gold photo corners

76 ivory 6mm freshwater pearls

Craft glue

Photo-safe glue stick

Fabric glue

Tools

Straight pins

Iron

Ironing board

Ruler

Scissors

Wooden stylus or craft stick

Gift scrapbooks are a thoughtful way to share special occasion or everyday photos. I like to decorate the cover with pretty ribbon and simple beading. I usually place a few finished pages inside to get the recipient started.

Instructions

1 Fold the Denim
Fold the long edges of the denim pieces back ¼", and pin them in place. Iron the fold, and remove the pins.

2 Attach the Denim to the Cover
Center the denim on the front of the cover. Wrap the ends around the top and bottom edges, and use fabric glue to attach them to the inside of the cover.

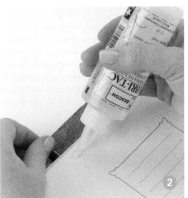

3 Attach the Ribbon to the Cover
Center the ribbon over the denim on the front of the cover. Wrap the ends around the top and bottom edges, and use fabric glue to attach them to the inside of the cover. Cut any dimensional accents off the ribbon that is attached to the inside of the cover.

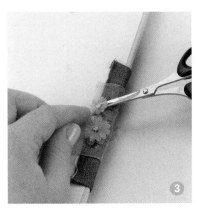

4 Cover the Denim and Ribbon Ends
Cut a piece of heavyweight paper to fit the inside of the cover. Use a glue stick to glue the paper over the inside of the cover to hide and protect the denim and ribbon ends.

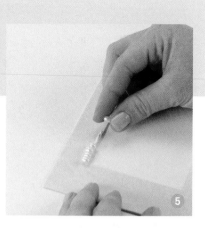

⑤ Decorate the Photo Mat

Use a wooden stylus or craft stick to make a 1" line of glue along the inside edge of the photo mat opening. Add a bit of glue if necessary to create a thick line. Add pearls one at a time to the glue. Gluing the pearls a section at a time prevents the glue from drying out as you work.

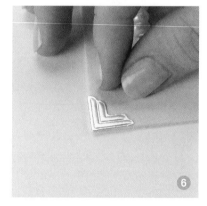

⑥ Apply the Photo Corners

Attach a photo corner to each corner of the mat. Allow the glue to dry completely, (this prevents glue getting on the photo).

⑦ Attach a Photo to the Mat

Turn the photo mat right side down. Use a glue stick to make a thin line of glue around the inside of the photo mat opening. Lay the photograph right side down on the glue. Turn the mat right side up, and use your fingers to carefully press down all over the mat to completely adhere the photo.

⑧ Glue the Mat to the Cover

Turn the photo mat right side down. Make a line of fabric glue above and below the edges of the photo. Glue the mat to the cover as shown.

Tip

Use three-dimensional accents to create your own decorative ribbon. Arrange the embellishments on a piece of wide ribbon, and then attach them with craft glue or simple stitching.

Embellished Scrapbook Page

Materials

2 white 1" cardstock
  squares per photo

1 teaspoon blue seed beads

1 tablespoon silver tiny marbles

½" double-sided adhesive tape

5 silver-rimmed ¾" round tags

20" silver 26-gauge craft wire

10" blue yarn

Tools

Scissors

6" piece of ⅛" wooden dowel

Wire cutters

Paper plate

Ruler

Beading adds dimension and sparkle to scrapbook pages. You can purchase nearly any kind of pre-made wire and bead embellishment, but it only takes a few easy techniques to create your own photo corners and beaded tags.

Craig and I spent two days in Paris during our European travels. One of my favorite parts of our visit was riding a giant Ferris wheel at sunset. We also saw the Arc de Triomphe and the Eiffel Tower and visited the Louvre.

Instructions

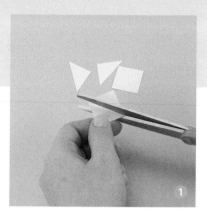

① Make Photo Corners
Cut the cardstock squares diagonally to create photo corners. Place a piece of double-sided adhesive tape on the back of the corners, but don't remove the paper backing until you're ready to attach them to the page.

② Add Beads to Photo Corners
Cover the front of each photo corner with double-sided adhesive tape. Place the corners on a paper plate. Sprinkle seed beads onto the photo corners, then dip into or sprinkle each corner with the tiny marbles.

③ Add Wire to a Tag
Cut a 2" piece of fuzzy yarn, and place it through the tag hole. Cut a 4" piece of wire. Place it through the tag hole, centered over the yarn. Wrap the wire loosely around the yarn to hold it in place.

④ Coil the Wire
Wrap the wire ends around a dowel to coil them. Refer to the instructions on page 27. Remove the dowel. Add a few beads. Use your fingers to press the last loop closed to prevent the beads from sliding off.

Tip
When making photo corners and embellishments, make at least twice as many as you need for this page. That way, the next time you need a sparkly page embellishment, you'll be all set.

Whimsical Beaded Bugs

Materials

3 turquoise 6mm firepolish beads

Green 8mm disk bead

Light blue 6mm round bead

Light blue 8mm fluted bead

2 green 12mm rectangle beads

2 turquoise 12mm diamond beads

4 turquoise size 6/0 seed beads

60 green size 11/0 seed beads

80 turquoise size 11/0 seed beads

200 assorted size 11/0 seed beads

Lengths of silver 24-gauge
  craft wire: 16" and 24"

Tools

Round nose pliers

Wire cutters

Ruler

*Add a colorful, cheery touch to gift packages with these beaded bugs.
They also can be used to make magnets, ornaments or jewelry.*

Instructions for the Dragonfly

① Make a Body

a. String a 6mm round bead onto the center of the 16" wire. Fold the wire in half.
b. Hold the ends together, and string a diamond-shaped bead and a rectangular bead.

② Make Lower Wings

String 30 green seed beads onto one wire above the rectangular bead. Bend it in a loop and twist the base to form a wing. Use the other wire to make a second lower wing. Twist the ends together once at the wire base.

③ Make Upper Wings

String 40 turquoise seed beads onto one end. Bend it in a loop, and twist the base to form a wing. Use the other wire end to make a second upper wing. Twist the ends together once at the wire base.

④ Bead the Head and Antennae

a. Hold the wires together and string an 8mm bead.
b. Cut the wire ends to 1½" to 1¾". Place a size 6/0 bead on the end of each wire. Use round nose pliers to loop the wire end around each bead. Use your fingers to bend each wire end in a spiral.

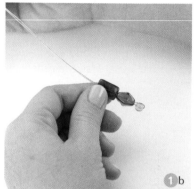

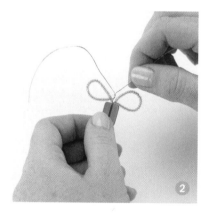

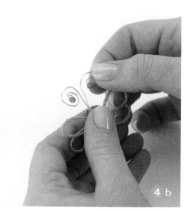

Instructions for the Butterfly

① Make a Body
String a 6mm bead onto the center of the wire. Fold the wire in half. Hold the ends together, and string another 6mm bead.

② Make Lower Wings
a. String 40 assorted turquoise and green seed beads onto one end. Bend it in a loop, and twist the base to form a wing. Use the other wire to make a second lower wing.
b. Twist the ends together once at the wire base. Hold the wires together, and string a 6mm bead.

③ Make Upper Wings
String 60 assorted turquoise and green seed beads onto one end. Bend it in a loop, and twist the base to form a wing. Use the other wire to make a second upper wing. Twist the ends together once at the wire base.

④ Bead the Head and Antennae
a. Hold the wires together, and string an 8mm bead.
b. Cut the wire ends to 1½" to 1¾". Place a size 6/0 bead on the end of each wire. Use round nose pliers to loop the wire end around each bead. Use your fingers to bend each wire end in a spiral.

Tip
Experiment with making other winged creatures, like bumblebees, fairies and angels. Attach a piece of nylon monofilament to hang your creation in a sunny window.

Glass Bottles

Materials for the Clear Bottle

5" clear glass bottle with cork

2 clear 6mm round glass beads

2 clear 8mm faceted glass beads

Clear 10mm faceted glass bead

1¼" glass drawer pull

12" silver 18-gauge craft wire

3 silver head pins

Extra-strength glue

Materials for the Blue Bottle

7" blue glass bottle with cork

2 blue 8mm faceted cat's eye beads

2 clear size 6/0 seed beads

Lengths of 18-gauge silver
  craft wire: 14" and 3"

5" silver 20-gauge craft wire

Extra-strength glue

Tools for Both Bottles

Round nose pliers

Wire cutters

Ruler

A friend gave me a bottle of dried lavender flowers from her garden and suggested that I keep it on my desk. When I'm frustrated, I sniff the flowers and instantly feel comforted. These bottles make pretty little packages for a small but mighty gesture of your own.

Instructions for the Clear Bottle

1 Wrap the Bottle
a. Use round nose pliers to make a loop on each end of the wire.
b. Make a four-turn spiral on one wire end. Hold the spiral against the front of the bottle, and wrap the wire tightly around the bottleneck.

2 Make Beaded Charms
a. String an 8mm bead onto a head pin. Use round nose pliers to make a loop above the bead.
b. Cut off any extra wire. Repeat for another head pin. Attach both charms to the outer loop on the spiral. String a 10mm bead and a 6mm bead on a head pin, make a loop, and attach the head pin between the other two beaded charms.

3 Decorate the Cork
Glue a glass drawer pull to the top of the cork. Glue a 6mm bead to the center of the drawer pull.

Instructions for the Blue Bottle

① Wrap the Bottle

Use round nose pliers to make a loop on each end of the 14" length of 18-gauge wire. Make a three-turn spiral on one wire end. Hold the spiral against the front of the bottle, and then wrap the wire tightly three times around the bottleneck.

② Make a Spiral Charm

Use round nose pliers to make a loop on one end of the 20-gauge wire. Make a three-turn spiral. Bend the wire end 90 degrees so it protrudes upward from the spiral.

③ Bead a Spiral Charm

String a 6/0 bead, an 8mm bead and a 6/0 bead onto the wire. Use round nose pliers to make a loop. Attach it to the outer loop spiral on the bottle front.

④ Decorate the Cork

Use the 3" length of 18-gauge wire to make a three-turn spiral. Bend the wire 90 degrees so it protrudes downward from the spiral. String an 8mm bead onto the wire. Place the wire end in the center of the cork to make a pilot hole. Remove it, add glue, and press it into the cork again.

Tip

Other sweet, small things to put in bottles:
Herbal tea blends
Bath salts
Dried flowers
Beads
Garden seeds

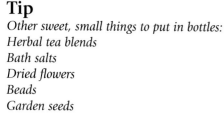

Patchwork Notebook

Materials

4¾" x 5½" white
  spiral-bound notebook

15 black 6mm aurora borealis
  finish, bicone glass beads

2 tablespoons purple iris seed beads

2 black 20mm buttons

1¼" x 3" gray suede

2¼" x 3" purple suede

4" square black leather

5 pieces 12" assorted purple fibers

Rubber stamps: "belle" block,
  pocket watch and pillow design

Metallic silver permanent inkpad

3½" x 5" white cardstock

Black beading thread

Craft glue

Dimensional glaze

Tools

Size 12 sharp beading needle

Beading scissors

Craft or straight-edge knife

Cutting mat

Ruler

I've just learned how to do basic bead embroidery, and now I want to put it on everything. This notebook is a good excuse to do a few practice stitches. I like to decorate little books like this one and give them to friends to use as reading journals or mini photo albums.

Instructions

① Stamp the Leather

Use silver ink to stamp one "belle," one pocket watch, and three to four pillow designs onto black leather, leaving ¼" between the designs.

② Cut the Leather Pieces

Use a craft knife and a cutting mat to cut out the "belle block," leaving a ¹⁄₁₆" border. Cut out the pocket watch, leaving a ⅛" to ¼" border. Cut a 3½" x 2" piece out of the pillow design stamped area. Cut a 1¼" x 3" piece of gray suede and a 2¼" x 3" piece of purple suede.

③ Assemble the Patchwork

Glue the gray and purple suede pieces side-by-side on one end of the patchwork. Glue the 3½" x 2" piece of black leather across the end of the suede pieces.

④ Add Seed Bead Stitches

Cut 10" of beading thread. Tie a knot in one end. Thread the needle onto the other end. Push the needle through the back of the cardstock near the gray/purple suede seam. Add four beads and stitch across the seam. Repeat for seven stitches as shown.

⑤ Add 6mm Bead Stitches

Cut 12" of beading thread. Tie a knot in one end. Thread the needle onto the other end. Push the needle through the back of the cardstock between the gray and black pieces. String a bicone bead onto the needle; stitch through the cardstock, then back through the bead. String two beads, and backstitch through the second bead. String the remaining beads, backstitching through every third bead.

⑥ Glue the Patchwork to the Cover

Spread an even layer of glue on the back of the cardstock. Press the patchwork onto the center of the front of the notebook cover.

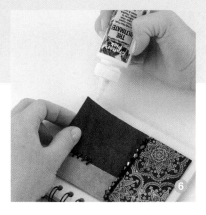

⑦ Attach other 3-D elements

Glue the "belle" block to the lower portion of the gray suede. Glue the pocket watch to the center of the purple suede. Glue one button to the center of the gray suede and another button above it.

⑧ Glue Seed Beads to the Cover

Use a craft stick to spread a thick line of glue along one edge of the patchwork. Sprinkle seed beads onto the glue. Repeat for each edge of the patchwork. Let the glue dry completely, and add glaze.

⑨ Attach Fibers to the Binding

String the fibers through the top ring on the spiral binding. Tie the whole bundle in an overhand knot. Tuck half the fibers through the second and third rings to hold the bundle in place.

Colorful Wine Charms

Materials

24 round 10mm faceted beads: 4 each color; turquoise, red, blue, green, purple, topaz

24 round 8mm faceted or bicone bead: 4 each color; turquoise, red, blue, green purple, topaz

24 round 6mm faceted bead: 4 each color; turquoise, red, blue, green, purple, topaz

24 round 4mm faceted or bicone bead: 4 each color; turquoise, red, blue, green, purple, topaz

6 silver beading hoops

24 silver head pins

12 silver 6mm jump rings

3" chain with lobster clasp

Tools

Round nose pliers

Chain nose pliers

Wire cutters

Want to show your hostess she's the most? Present her with a set of wine charms to use at her next party. The charms make a pretty decoration for a gift bottle of wine, plus, guests will be able to tell which glass is theirs.

Instructions to Make One Wine Charm

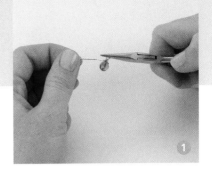

1 Make a Beaded Charm

String a 6mm bead onto a head pin. Use round nose pliers to make a loop above the bead. Wrap the extra wire around the base of the loop.

2 Attach a Charm to the Hoop

Use chain nose pliers to open a jump ring and connect it to the loop above the 6mm bead. Attach the jump ring to the beading hoop.

3 Attach an 8mm Bead

String an 8mm bead onto a head pin. Make a loop, attach it to the 6mm bead, and wrap the wire two to three times around the base of the loop. Cut off any extra wire.

4 Attach a 4mm Bead

String a 4mm bead onto a head pin. Make a loop, attach it to the 8mm bead, and then wrap the wire two to three times around the base of the loop. Cut off any extra wire.

5 Attach a 10mm Bead

String a 10mm bead onto a head pin. Make a loop and wrap the wire two to three times around the base of the loop. Cut off any extra wire. Connect the loop to a jump ring. Attach the jump ring on the 10mm beaded charm to the loop above the 8mm bead.

6 Attach the Wine Charm to the Chain

Open the beading hoop and attach it to a link on the chain. Bend the end of the beading hoop in a 90-degree angle, and place it through the loop to fasten it. To decorate a wine bottle and display the wine charms, wrap the chain around the neck.

Tip

For a quick and easy version: String a 10mm bead onto a head pin. Make a loop above the top bead, and attach it to a beading hoop.

Bejeweled Ornaments

Materials for All Ornaments

3 papier maché 4" ornaments

3 tablespoons each; red, gold, turquoise seed bead mix

3 tablespoons each; red, gold, turquoise mini marbles

1 teaspoon each; red, gold, turqoise very fine glitter

1 oz. each; red, yellow, turquoise acrylic paint

3 each; red, yellow, turquoise size "E" beads

3 pieces of 2" gold 26-gauge craft wire

3 pieces 24" to 36" gold 18-gauge craft wire

Craft glue

Dimensional glaze

Tools

1" paintbrush

Old bristle paintbrush

Craft stick

Round nose pliers

Wire cutters

Ruler

These sparkly ornaments were inspired by a set that my sister uses for year-round decorating. She hangs them from the bottoms of bookshelves to add a festive touch to her home. They are reminders to celebrate each and every day.

Instructions for Each Ornament

1 Paint the Ornament

Use the 1" paintbrush to paint an even coat of paint onto one side of the ornament. Let it dry, then paint the other side. Paint the edges.

2 Attach the Beads

a. Use a craft stick to spread a thick layer of glue onto one side of the ornament. Sprinkle beads, mini marbles and glitter onto the ornament. Let the glue dry completely.
b. Use an old bristle paintbrush to apply sealer to the front of the ornament. Let it dry. Seal the edges and the back.

3 Make a Spiral

a. Use round nose pliers to make a loop on each end of the craft wire.
b. Hold the loop between your thumb and forefinger, and turn your wrist to create a loose spiral shape on each wire end.

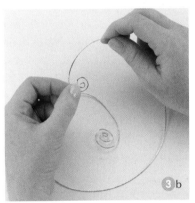

4 Wire-wrap the Ornament

Hold one spiral on the front of the ornament, and wrap the wire around the ornament several times. Use round nose pliers to kink the wire on the back of the ornament. This will tighten the wire and hold it in place.

5 String Beads onto the Hanger

Place a piece of 26-gauge wire through the gold cord hanger, and fold it in half. Twist the wire together. Use it as a needle to string three size "E" beads onto the cord. Cut the wire, and remove it from the cord.

Tip

To personalize the ornament, use wire to spell out a name. Attach one end of the name to the cord.

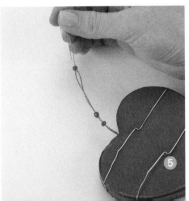

Two Gifts in One Bracelet Bouquet

Materials

5" glass vase with narrow neck

17 orange 10mm round glass beads

17 metal charms

9" white size .032" (0.80mm)
 transparent stretchy beading cord

Jeweler's cement

White acrylic paint

Tools

Scissors

Paper towels

Ruler

*No watering is required for this cheerful desktop flower arrangement.
Plus, the beaded embellishment is actually a bracelet.*

Instructions

1 Paint the Vase
Pour several large drops of white acrylic paint inside the vase. Shake and roll the vase so the paint covers the glass. Add more paint if necessary.

2 Drain the Vase
Place the vase upside-down on paper towels to allow any extra paint to drain out. Change the paper towels every few minutes until there is no more extra paint. Set the vase upright to finish air-drying.

3 String the Bracelet
String alternating beads and charms onto the elastic cord.

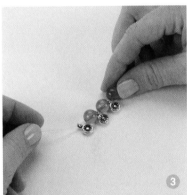

4 Tie the Ends
Tie the ends in a square knot. Place a drop of glue on the knot. Let the glue dry, and cut off any extra cord.

5 Finish the Vase
Place the bracelet on the vase as shown. Place flowers inside the vase.

Tip
This vase is meant for artificial flowers only. For fresh flowers, use special glass paints, or do not paint the inside of the vase.

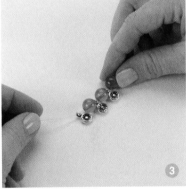

Bedazzling Bookmark

Materials

14" of size .015" (.038mm)
  49-strand flexible beading wire

240 size 11/0 lavender aurora
  borealis finish seed beads

Silver 12mm "Believe" bead

4 dark amethyst 6mm round beads

Light amethyst 4mm round bead

2 light purple 10mm
  round faceted glass beads

8 silver 6mm bead caps

2 decorative silver head pins

Silver eye pin

2 silver 1.3mm crimp beads

Tools

Wire cutters

Round nose pliers

Crimping tool

Ruler

This project combines two of my favorite things: beads and books. I often share copies of my most treasured books with friends and family. Including a pretty handmade bookmark makes my gifts even more personal.

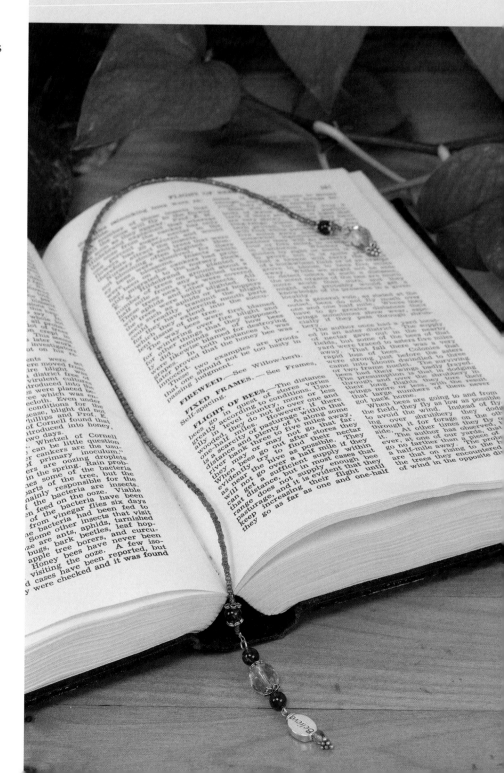

Instructions

1 Cut the Beading Wire

Cut a piece of wire 2" longer than the height of the book. If you're unsure of the book dimensions, 14" is a good general length.

2 Loop the End of the Beading Wire

String a crimp bead onto one end of the wire. Fold the other end, and place it inside the crimp bead to form a loop. Use a crimping tool to crimp the crimp bead. Refer to the crimping instructions on page 26.

3 Add Beads to the Beading Wire

String two seed beads onto the flexible beading wire. String a bead cap, 6mm bead and bead cap onto the wire. String seed beads to cover the wire except for the last 1½". String a bead cap, 6mm bead, bead cap and a crimp bead onto the wire end. Loop, and crimp the end as in Step 2.

4 Make a Single-Beaded Charm

String a bead cap, 10mm bead and bead cap onto a decorative head pin. Use round nose pliers to make a loop above the upper bead cap. Place one end of the bookmark inside the wire loop, then wrap the wire two to three times around the base of the loop. Cut off any extra wire.

5 Make the First Part of a Double-Beaded Charm

String the following beads onto an eye pin: dark amethyst 6mm, bead cap, light purple 10mm faceted, bead cap and dark amethyst 6mm. Use round nose pliers to make a loop next to the last bead, and cut off any excess wire. Attach it to the end of the bookmark.

6 Make the Second Part of a Double-Beaded Charm

String a light amethyst 4mm bead and the "Believe" bead onto a decorative head pin. Use round nose pliers to make a loop above the silver bead. Connect the loop to the eye pin on the other beaded charm. Wrap the extra wire around the base of the loop.

Tip

This is a great project for using leftover beads, or what is commonly known as "bead soup." Choose beads in the same color family or create your own mixture. Add a special charm to further personalize your creation.

Dragonfly Journal

Materials

5½" x 8½" linen-covered journal

4" x 9½" blue mulberry paper

9½" purple 1⅜" moiré ribbon

Embossed pewter 2"
  dragonfly sticker

1 teaspoon blue/purple
  seed bead mix

2 tablespoons silver tiny marbles

Dimensional glaze

Tools

Paper plate

Old paintbrush

Ruler

Double-sided tape

Tip

*Create a simple fabric
cover for any journal:
Open the journal, and measure it
crosswise and lengthwise. Add ½" to
the long edges and ¾" to the short
edges. Cut a piece of fabric to fit those
dimensions. Measure the width of the
binding and the distance from the
binding to the edge of the cover, then
cut a notch. Miter the corners, then fold
and glue all of the edges to the inside
of the cover. Cover the fabric edges by
gluing the first and last pages of the
journal or pieces of patterned paper to
the inside of the cover.*

*Journals make great gifts, because they tell the recipient that you think
she has something important to say. I'm drawn to dragonflies, because
they're symbols of regeneration. That's a fitting embellishment for a
blank book that is about to become someone's story, don't you think?*

Instructions

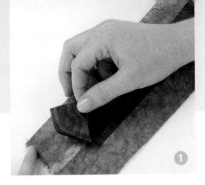

① Attach the Ribbon

Place double-sided tape lengthwise on the center of the paper. Attach the ribbon.

② Attach the Sticker

a. Remove the backing from the sticker and press it onto the ribbon, about 2⅛" from the upper edge.

b. Cut two 2¾" lengths of double-sided tape, and place them along the upper and lower edges of the sticker. Remove the paper backing. Cut two 2¼" lengths of double-sided tape, and place them along the sides of the sticker, overlapping the other pieces of tape. Remove the paper backing.

③ Add Seed Beads

Sprinkle mixed seed beads onto the tape. For this project, I wanted a lot of the silver to show through, so I sprinkled the seed beads sparingly onto the tape. For a denser beaded look, sprinkle beads more heavily onto the tape. Tap any extra beads onto a paper plate, and return them to the container.

④ Add Tiny Marbles

Sprinkle tiny marbles onto the beaded area to fill any spaces between the beads. Tap any extra marbles onto a paper plate, and return them to the container. Use the old paintbrush to spread glaze sparingly onto the beaded area. Make sure that the glaze doesn't spread onto the paper or ribbon, because it will discolor them.

⑤ Attach the Mulberry Paper

a. Use a glue stick to apply glue to the back of the mulberry paper along the upper ½" edge. Place the mulberry paper centered on the journal cover. Wrap the upper edge to the inside of the cover. Measure the edges to make sure the paper is straight, and wrap the lower edge to the inside.

b. Use your fingers to press the paper firmly against the inside of the cover. Use a glue stick to spread glue evenly over the first page of the journal. Press the first page against the inside of the journal cover to hide the paper and ribbon ends.

Blooming Bud Vase

My mom keeps a pretty little bud vase in her kitchen window. In the spring and summer, it holds bright blooms from her flower garden. In the winter, she adds artificial blooms for a bit of cold-weather cheer.

Materials

4¼" clear glass bottle

Copper 16-gauge
  wire: 1 each; 28", 18",
  8", (2) pieces 3"

Magenta 15mm
  plastic bicone bead

Purple 15mm
  plastic round bead

Tools

Round nose pliers

Wire cutters

Ruler

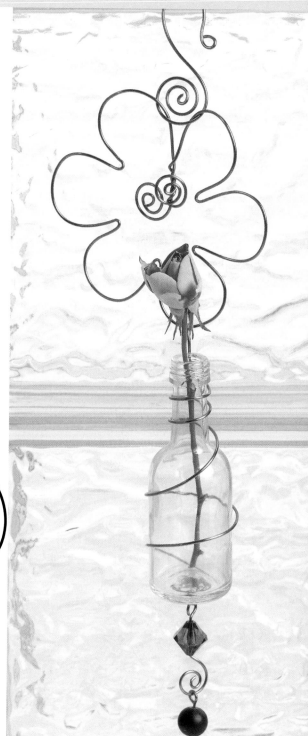

Actual Size Pattern for Step 2

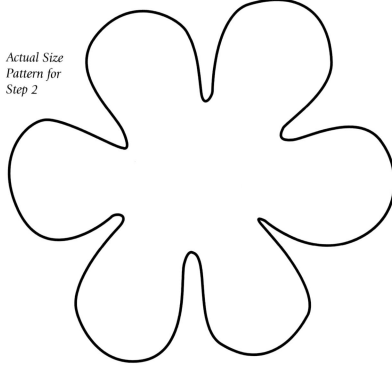

Instructions

① Spiral the Wire Ends
Use round nose pliers to make a loop on one end of all five pieces of wire. Hold a loop between your thumb and forefinger, and turn your wrist to make a spiral. Make three-turn spirals on the end of each wire.

② Begin the Flower
Lay the 28" wire over the pattern, and use your fingers to form the first petal. Use round nose pliers to make the bend to start the next petal.

③ Finish the Flower
When all of the petals are formed, make a spiral on the wire end. Twist the two spirals together in the flower center.

④ Wrap the Bottle
Hold the spiral on the end of the 18" wire firmly against the bottom of the bottle, and wrap the wire upward around the bottle.

⑤ Attach the Bottle
Use round nose pliers to make a loop on the end. Attach the loop to the bottom of the flower.

⑥ Make a Hook
Use your fingers to bend the 8" wire in an "S" shape. Use round nose pliers to make a loop on the end. String the spiral onto the top of the flower.

⑦ Make the Beaded Charms
String a bead onto a 3" wire. Use round nose pliers to make a loop. Cut off any extra wire. Repeat this step to make two beaded charms.

⑧ Attach the Beaded Charms
a. Fold the center loop on the bottom of the bottle downward to make a hanging loop for the charms.
b. Attach one charm to the loop. Connect the other charm to the lowest spiral.

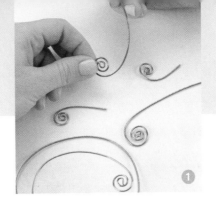

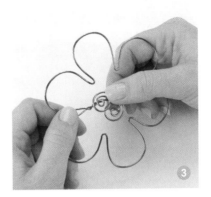

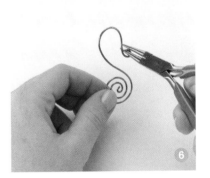
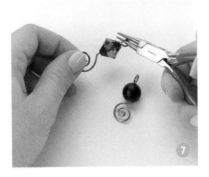
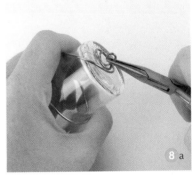
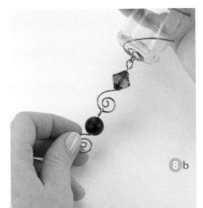

Sassy Photo Tote

Materials

8½" x 5" photo organizer with handles

7⅝" pink ⅝" daisy ribbon

7⅝" pink beaded trim

75 assorted pink plastic beads

28" black 26-gauge craft wire

Double-sided adhesive tape

Tools

Wire cutters

Scissors

Ruler

Photos make great gifts—especially when they're completely organized and ready to scrapbook. With a few extra embellishments, a stylish file makes the perfect presentation for your shared memories.

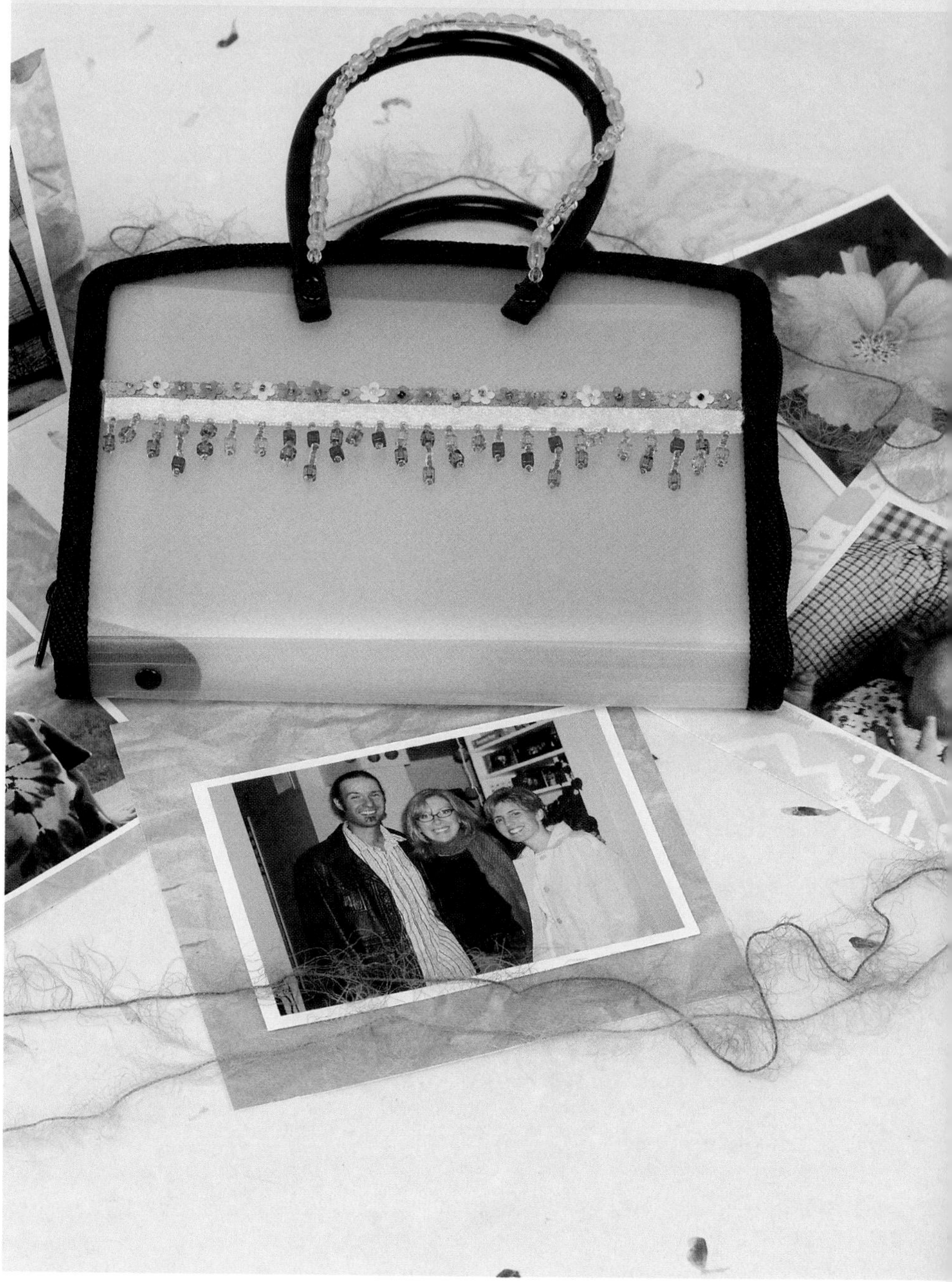

Instructions

① Attach Beaded Trim

Place a piece of double-sided adhesive tape across the front of the photo tote, about 3½" from the bottom edge. Press beaded trim onto the adhesive.

② Attach Embroidered Ribbon

Place a piece of double-sided adhesive tape across the top of the beaded trim. Press embroidered ribbon onto the adhesive.

③ Bead the Handle

a. Cut a 24" length of wire. Place the center of the wire at the base of one handle. Wrap it around the handle from back to front.
b. Hold the wires together, and randomly string all of the beads.

④ Fasten the Beaded Handle

After the last bead, wrap the wires to the back of the handle, and twist them together. Cut off any extra wire. Cut two 2" wire pieces. Wrap one piece of wire around the beaded wire and the handle between the 12th and 13th bead from the handle base. Repeat on the other side of the handle.

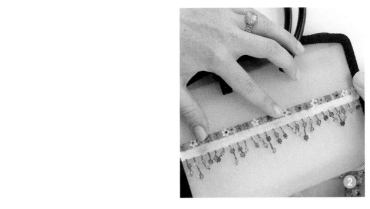

Tip

You can use a similar technique to embellish ordinary photo brag books. Punch holes in the covers where the handles should attach. Set an eyelet in each hole. To make handles, attach sheer ribbon or beaded cord. Add beaded trim and embroidered ribbon to the front.

Mini Frame Trio

Materials and Tools for All of the Frames

3 white satin 3" x 4" picture frames

Circle crest rubber stamp

Craft glue

Straight pin

Wooden stylus or craft stick

Pencil

Heat tool or hair dryer

Scissors

Ruler

Materials for the Purple Frame

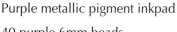

Purple metallic pigment inkpad

40 purple 6mm beads
 in assorted shapes

Materials for the Teal Frame

Teal metallic pigment inkpad

144 teal size 6/0 seed beads

White cardstock

Materials for the Black Frame

Black metallic pigment inkpad

120 black size 6/0 seed beads

Okay, I'll admit it. I can't get enough of my family's vintage photos, or any vintage photos for that matter. And these little frames are the perfect size for gift giving. Tuck a special photo into one, and pass it along to a family member or friend.

Instructions for Each Frame

① Stamp the Image onto the Frame

Ink a rubber stamp with metallic ink. Press the stamp onto the frame. Re-ink the rubber stamp, and stamp it again, until the entire frame is covered.

② Heat-set the Ink

Some inkpads take longer to dry on fabric than others. To speed the drying time, use a heat tool or hair dryer to heat-set the ink.

③ Add Beads to the Purple Frame

Use a wooden stylus or craft stick to spread a thick line of glue around half of the oval picture frame. Work with one section at a time to prevent the glue from drying while you work. Press a single line of beads into the glue.

④ Create a Corner Template for the Teal Frame

Cut a 1" square of white cardstock. Cut the square in half diagonally to create a corner template. Lay the corner template on one of the picture frame corners. Use a sharp pencil to draw a line along the diagonal edge of the corner template.

⑤ Add Beads to the Teal Frame

Use a wooden stylus or craft stick to spread a thick layer of glue over the pencil line and into the corner. String one row of teal beads onto the straight pin. (The straight pin helps keep the beads in line). Place the row of beads in the glue along the diagonal edge. Remove the pin. String one row at a time onto the pin. As you lay the beads in the glue, you'll be able to adjust the spacing and straighten the lines. Repeat two more times as shown, for each corner.

⑥ Add Beads to the Black Frame

Use a wooden stylus or craft stick to spread a thick line of glue along one outside edge of the frame. String black beads onto a straight pin. Place them in the glue along the edge of the frame. As you lay the beads in the glue, you'll be able to adjust and straighten the lines.

Tip

Can't find an appropriate anniversary gift? Frame a vintage family photo for the happy couple.

Royal Pet Collar

Materials

Black pet collar

1 yd. black size .011"
  (.028mm) beading thread

10 pink 6mm plastic rondelle beads

10 pink 4mm plastic faceted beads

10 pink 8mm plastic faceted beads

10 pink 9mm plastic tube beads

10 pink 6mm plastic round beads

Silver/pink crown charm

1 each; 4mm and 6mm
  silver jump rings

Tools

Size 12 hard beading needle

Needle threader

Chain nose pliers

Beading scissors

My cats both are going to be even more spoiled now that I'm making them beaded collars. This makes a nice gift for the person who has everything. You can treat your friend's best friend!

Instructions

1 **Sew the First Stitch**

Thread the needle, and knot the thread end. Position the needle next to the buckle. Stitch from the lower edge of the back of the collar to the front.

2 **Stitch the First Row**

Add a tube bead, and stitch back through the upper edge of the collar.

3 **Attach the Second Row**

Bring the thread horizontally along the upper edge, and stitch through to the front of the collar. String an 8mm faceted bead, and stitch back through the lower edge of the collar.

4 **Add the Remaining Beads**

Use the sewing techniques from Steps 2 and 3 to add the remaining beads to the collar. Follow this beading pattern: one 9mm tube bead, one 8mm faceted, two 4mm faceted, one 6mm round and two rondelles.

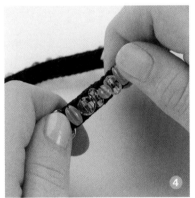

5 **Knot the Thread End**

Stitch the end of the thread to make a knot. Cut off any extra thread.

6 **Attach a Charm**

Use chain nose pliers to open a 4mm jump ring, and attach it to the charm. Connect a 6mm jump ring to the 4mm jump ring. Attach the 6mm jump ring to the collar.

Tip

You can use any assortment of beads to create a beaded pet collar. Attach the beads randomly to the collar, or create your own beading pattern. For a quick and easy version, use glue to attach beads to the collar.

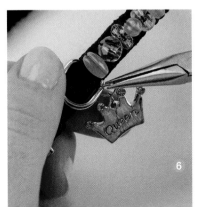

Simple but Stunning Cards

Materials

Found on individual project pages

Tools for All of the Cards

Round nose pliers

Chain nose pliers

Wire cutters

Paper trimmer or
  straight edge craft knife

Craft stick (to apply glue)

Round nose pliers

Ruler

Basic Card Making Instructions

Layer all of the paper elements
on a card as shown in the photo.
Use a glue stick to attach paper
to paper on the heart and flower
cards. For the spiral card, attach
double-sided tape to the back of
the paper strips, and use them to
attach the vellum pieces to the card.
(Glue can make vellum buckle.)

I've been making handmade cards for a long time, and it seems that sometimes the recipient appreciates a special card even more than the gift itself. Attach wire and bead accents to simple paper collages to make easy, distinctive cards.

Materials for the Heart Card

10" gold 26-gauge craft wire

230 silver-lined size 15/0 seed beads

5" x 6½" ivory blank card

2" square of gold cardstock

2½" square of
 ivory glimmer cardstock

Craft glue

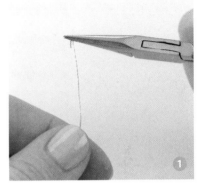

Instructions for the Beaded Heart

① Fold the Ends
Use chain nose pliers to fold one end of the wire ⅛", and press the wires together. This will prevent beads from sliding off the end of the wire.

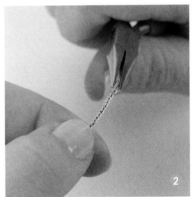

② String Beads onto the Wire
String beads onto the wire, using the wire end to pick up beads. When only ¼" of uncovered wire is left, fold the end over ⅛". The extra space will allow beads to float freely on the wire when you form the heart.

③ Form the Heart
a. Fold the wire in half, then cross the ends to make a center loop.
b. Turn the loop over. Use your fingers to shape the shoulders of the heart, and twist the wires together.

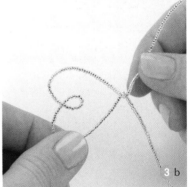

④ Form the Spirals
Use round nose pliers to grasp the wire end (not the beads) to make a loop on one wire end. Place the loop between your thumb and forefinger, and turn your wrist to make a spiral. Repeat for the other wire end.

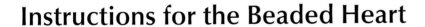

Materials for the Daisy Card

3 pieces 10" silver
  28-gauge craft wire

3 pink 5mm buttons

100 white size 11/0 seed beads

4" white blank card

1¾" x 3¼" burgundy cardstock

3¼" square burgundy/white
  patterned paper

Craft glue

Wire cutter

Instructions for One Beaded Daisy

1 String the Button onto the Wire
Place both wire ends through the button from front to back.
Pull the ends even so the button is centered on the wire. Twist
the ends together once to hold the button in place.

2 Make a Petal
Use the wire end to pick up 20 white seed beads. Hold the
first and last bead together, and twist to form a petal.

3 Make a Petal
Use the other wire to pick up beads, and twist together
to form a petal as in Step 2. Repeat making petals with
alternating ends of the wire until five petals are formed.

4 Finish the Daisy
Once all of the petals are formed, twist the ends together, and cut
off any excess wire. Glue the daisy to the front of the card.

Materials for the Spiral Card

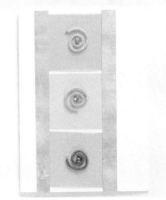

4" silver 26-gauge craft wire

60 each, purple, blue, green
 size 11/0 seed beads

3 silver mini brads

5" x 6½" ivory blank card

1 each; purple, blue, green
 ⅞" x 2" piece of vellum

2 purple ½" x 5" patterned papers

Double-sided adhesive tape

Glue stick

Instructions for the Beaded Spiral

1 String Beads onto the Wire
Use chain nose pliers to fold one end of the wire ⅛", and press the wires together. This will prevent beads from sliding off the end of the wire. String beads onto the wire, using the wire end to pick up beads.

2 Loop the Wire End
When only ¼" of uncovered wire is left, use round nose pliers to form a loop on the wire end.

3 Form the Spiral
Place the loop between your thumb and forefinger, and turn your wrist to make a spiral.

4 Attach a Brad to the Spiral
Place a brad through the loop to attach the spiral to the vellum piece.

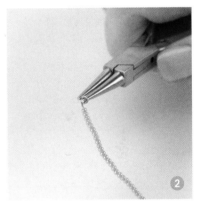

Chapter 4: Home Decor

Beaded accents add a touch of sparkle and style to every room in your home. The projects in this chapter will show you how to create your own personalized decorator look. Change the project's colors to coordinate with your décor, or become inspired to create a whole new look.

Carriage Clock

Materials

Unfinished wooden carriage clock

150 blue 4mm to 8mm
firepolish glass beads

1½" glass drawer pull

6½" square blue/
white patterned paper

Adhesive clock face

Clock movement

2 oz. white acrylic paint

Satin acrylic liquid sealer

Glue for glass and metal

Dimensional glaze

Decoupage gel

Tools

Sandpaper

1" bristle paintbrush

1" foam paintbrush

Craft stick

Small scissors

*Besides being a pretty accent piece for your home, this clock
will remind you that there's always time to bead. The cool
blue shades remind me of summertime at the beach.*

Instructions

① Prepare the Wood
Follow the instructions on page 29 for preparing unfinished wooden items.

② Paint the Clock
Paint the clock white. Seal the clock, except for the center (where the face will attach) and the sides (where the beads will attach).

③ Attach Paper to the Clock
Use a foam paintbrush to spread a thin layer of gel onto the center of the clock and on the back of the paper. Working from one side to the other, place the patterned paper on the center of the clock and smooth it with your fingers.

④ Decoupage the Clock
Use the foam paintbrush to spread a thin layer of gel over the front of the patterned paper. Use your fingers to press out any air bubbles. Let the gel dry.

⑤ Attach the Beads
a. Use a craft stick to spread a thick layer of glass and metal glue onto a 2" area on one side of the clock as shown.
b. Press a few beads into the glue. Working with a small area at a time helps prevent the glue from drying. Glue beads to the other side of the clock. When dry, apply a thin layer of dimensional glaze.

⑥ Attach the Drawer Pull
Use glass and metal glue to attach a glass drawer pull to the center of the top of the clock.

⑦ Attach the Clock Face
Use small scissors to cut out the circle in the center of the clock. Remove the adhesive backing from the clock face, and attach it to the center of the clock.

⑧ Assemble the Clock Movement
Place the clock movement through the hole in the center of the clock. Assemble it as directed on the package.

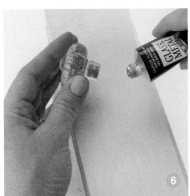

Beaded Accent Lamp

Materials

14" white candlestick-style
  lamp base

4" x 11" x 7½" white
  linen lampshade

15 clear 12mm firepolish beads

44" clear beaded trim

22" maribou feather trim

8" clear size .032" (.80mm)
  stretchy beading cord

Fabric glue

Glue for glass and metal

Tools

Scissors

Clothespins

Ruler

Sparkly beaded trim turns any ordinary lamp into a stylish home accent. Keep it simple with monochromatic beaded trim, or add feathers for a more whimsical touch.

Instructions

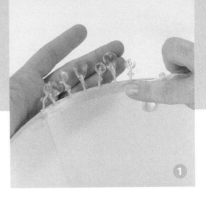

❶ Attach Beaded Trim to the Shade
Turn the lampshade upside down. Starting at the back of the shade, place a 6" line of fabric glue along the inside edge of the shade. Press the beaded trim into the glue. Continue adding glue and beaded trim until the ends meet. Cut off any extra beaded trim, and set it aside for Step 2. Let the glue dry.

❷ Attach Beaded Trim to the Base
Make a thin line of glass and metal glue around the base of the candlestick. Starting at the back, press the beaded trim into the glue.

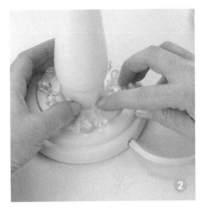

❸ Attach Feather Trim to the Shade
Make a thick line of fabric glue around the upper edge of the shade about ½" from the top. Starting at the back of the shade, press the feather trim into the glue. Cut off any extra feather trim, and set it aside for Step 4. Clip clothespins to the trim and lampshade to hold the trim in place while the glue dries.

❹ Attach Feather Trim to the Base
Make a thick line of glass and metal glue around the candlestick neck so it will show just below the lower edge of the lampshade. Press the feather trim into the glue. Use a clothespin to hold the ends together while the glue dries.

❺ Add Beads to the Base
String the firepolish beads onto a piece of stretchy beading cord. Wrap the cord around the base of the candlestick, and tie the ends in a square knot. Cut off any extra cord.

Tip
This basic lamp base and shade can change dramatically, depending on the color of the shade. Using white feather trim and clear beaded trim keeps it clean and contemporary.
Classic Vintage—black shade with amber beads
Girlie Girl— pink or purple shade with matching beads
Cottage Chic—pastel yellow or light green shade with matching beads

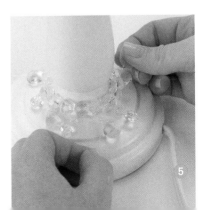

Shabby Chic Mirror

Materials

½" x 12" x 12" craft plywood

4" square bevel-edged mirror

80 pink 6mm firepolish glass beads

2½ yd. silver 26-gauge craft wire

9½" square green/pink floral
  patterned paper

2 oz. ivory acrylic paint

Satin acrylic liquid sealer

4 silver wire ½" brad nails

Sawtooth hanger and nails

Decoupage gel

Glue for glass and metal

Tools

Sandpaper

1" paintbrush

Ruler

Pencil

Chain nose pliers

6" piece of ⅛" wooden dowel

Wire cutters

Hammer

Tip
Change the patterned paper to completely change the look of this mirror. Use checked print for a girl's bedroom, red/white cherries for a cheery kitchen or blue/white toile for a cottage living room.

Decoupage is back! Pretty patterned paper makes this mirror a snap. Add some wire and beads to the edges for extra pizzazz. Placing a mirror across from your doorway is supposed to bring good luck to the house.

Instructions

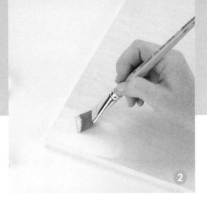

1 **Prepare the Wood**
Refer to the instructions on page 29 for preparing unfinished wooden items.

2 **Paint the Wood**
Paint the plywood ivory. Let the paint dry thoroughly between coats. Apply a coat of sealer.

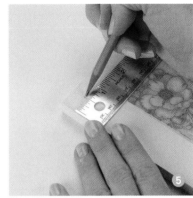

3 **Attach the Paper**
Spread a thin layer of decoupage glue over the wrong side of the paper, and place it on the center of the plywood square. Apply decoupage glue on the right side of the paper and the plywood edges. Let it dry.

4 **Attach the Sawtooth Hanger**
Place the sawtooth hanger at the center of the upper edge on the back of the wood. Position it ½" below the upper edge. Use nails to attach the hanger.

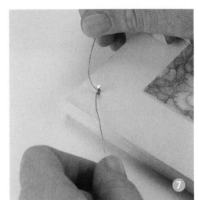

5 **Mark the Wood**
On each corner of the plywood, measure in ½" from both sides. Make a light pencil mark to show where the nails will be attached.

6 **Attach the Nails**
Use chain nose pliers to hold a nail in place on the pencil mark. Hammer the nails in place.

7 **Attach the Wire**
Wrap one wire end two times around one nail.

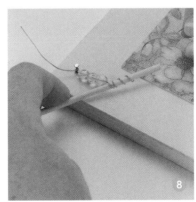

8 **Add Beads**
String beads onto the wire, coil the wire 4 to 5 times around a dowel, and string more beads. Use the following pattern: three beads, coil, one bead, coil, two beads and coil; repeat. Wrap the wire one full time around each nail.

9 **Secure the Wire**
Wrap the wire end two to three times around the last nail to hold the wire in place. Cut off any extra wire.

10 **Attach the Mirror**
Lay the mirror diagonally in the center of the patterned paper. Measure to make sure it is in the center. Use a pencil to lightly mark the lower corner. Spread glue on the back of the mirror, and place it in the center of the patterned paper.

Vintage Pillow Cover

Materials:

12" canvas pillow cover

180 rose 6mm firepolish beads

2 yd. white size .008" (.20mm) beading thread

Passport collage rubber stamp

4" x 6" light brown doeskin leather

Black permanent inkpad

Metallic permanent inkpads: gold-blue, gold-violet, indigo, sepia, gold-red

Fabric glue

Tools

Small paintbrush

Size 12 beading needle

Needle threader

Beading scissors

Straight-edge craft knife

Cutting mat

Optional: hair dryer or heat tool

Ruler

Tip
Use a hair dryer or heat tool to speed drying time and to make heat-set inks permanent.

For a modern take on a vintage look, create this stamped and beaded pillow cover. Use the same techniques with different rubber stamps to make a unique collection of decorative pillows.

Instructions

1 Stamp the Central Image

Ink the stamp with black ink, and place it with the image side down on the leather. Press firmly on the stamp without rocking it. For large stamps like this one, I like to place a large book on top of the stamp and then press down. The book distributes the pressure more evenly over the image.

2 Cut the Leather

a. Use a straight-edge craft knife to cut out the central image. By stamping the image first, you can be sure it will be centered on the leather.
b. Cut two 2" squares. Cut them diagonally to create corners.

3 Stamp the Corners

Ink one corner of the rubber stamp with black ink. Stamp the image onto a leather corner. Repeat for each corner.

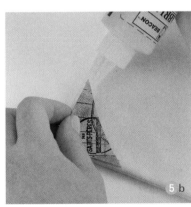

4 Paint the Leather Pieces

Use a small paintbrush to apply ink from the metallic inkpads to different areas of the stamped images as shown. The compass is painted indigo, the upper right butterfly is gold-red, the lower butterfly is gold-violet, the passport is gold-blue, and the postmark is sepia. Paint the leather corner backgrounds gold-violet.

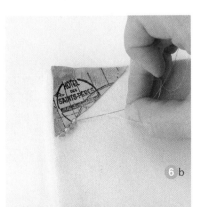

5 Attach the Leather Pieces

a. Use fabric glue to attach the large image to the center of the pillow cover.
b. Glue a leather corner to each corner of the pillow cover.

6 Attach the Beads

a. Thread the needle, knot the thread end, and stitch through the pillow cover near the large, stamped image. Add beads, stitching back through every fourth or fifth bead.
b. Use the same technique to add beads to the pillow corners.

Simple Beaded Basket

Materials

5" x 7" x 5½" basket with lid

16 natural 12mm wooden beads

15 light brown
   10mm wooden beads

22 dark brown
   10mm wooden beads

2" brown leather rose pin

Lengths of 20 lb. test hemp
   cord: 4 yd. pieces (2)
   and 2 yd. piece (1)

Craft glue

Glue for glass and metal

Tools

Beading scissors

Macramé board or clipboard

Tip

For an even quicker version of this basket, glue store-bought beaded trim to the basket instead of creating your own macramé trim.

Use beads and other embellishments to give a plain but pretty basket a stylish makeover. I use baskets throughout the house to store everything from toiletries to board games to craft supplies. Adding a little beading makes a basket fun in addition to functional.

Instructions

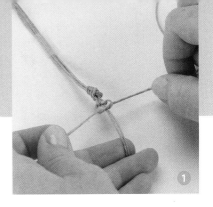

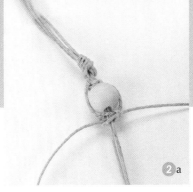

1 Tie the Cords Together

Hold the lengths of hemp cord together in the center. Leave about 4" on the end, and then tie an overhand knot. Attach the knot to your macramé board or clipboard.

2 Make a Beaded Section

a. String a natural bead onto the inner strands. Use the outer strands to tie a square knot around the inner strands.
b. Tying square knots between each bead, string a dark brown bead, a natural brown bead and a light brown bead.

3 String a Double-Bead Section

String a dark brown bead onto each outside strand. Tie the outer strands in a square knot.

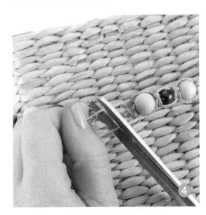

4 Tie the Ends

Repeat the bead/knot pattern in Steps 2 and 3 until the beaded piece is long enough to wrap around the basket. Wrap the beaded piece around the basket. Tie the ends together. Add a drop of glue. When the glue is dry, cut off any extra cord.

5 Attach the Beads to the Basket

a. Cut six 2" to 3" pieces of hemp cord. Lay one piece of cord over the beaded piece, and place the cord ends through the front of the basket.
b. Tie the cord ends together inside the basket to hold the beaded piece in place. Space the cords evenly over the length of the beaded piece.

6 Glue the Flower to the Basket

Place a quarter-sized drop of glue on the back of the flower. Glue it to the center front rim of the lid.

Sparkly Sun Catcher

Materials

1¾" glass prism

14 grams blue/silver seed bead/ bugle bead mix

Blue 6mm glass cat's eye bead

Clear 8mm faceted rondelle bead

3 turquoise 8mm bicone beads

2 clear 8mm faceted teardrops

Loop of necklace-size memory wire

Lengths of silver 18-gauge craft wire: 6" and 1½"

4 blue/silver 6" lengths of assorted fibers

Extra-strength glue

Tools

Round nose pliers

Wire cutters

Scissors

Ruler

Tip

Make a quick and easy version: Tie a glass prism to one end of a piece of flexible beading wire. String beads to cover the wire except for the last 2". Fold the end, and tie the wires in an overhand knot above the last bead to make a loop for hanging the sun catcher.

A prism in the window creates a nice focus for daydreaming and sheds tiny rainbows on the room—what could be better? This sun catcher's shape was inspired by the Native American dream catchers that I saw on a recent trip to Colorado.

Instructions

① Bead the Wire
String seed bead/bugle bead mix to cover the necklace wire except for the last ¼".

② Glue the Wire Ends
Place a drop of glue on both ends of the wire and place them inside a bugle bead. Let the glue dry.

③ Attach the Fibers
Fold the fibers in half over the glued wire ends. Cut 3" off one of the fibers, and use it to tie the fibers together just below the fold.

④ Attach the Prism
a. Use round nose pliers to make a large loop on one end of the 1½" piece of wire.
b. String the prism onto the loop. String a cat's eye bead, a rondelle and a bicone bead onto the wire. Loop the end.
c. Use chain nose pliers to open the loop sideways, and slip it onto the beaded memory wire. Do not close the loop until Step 5.

⑤ Make a Hanger
a. Make a loop on one end of the 6" wire. Place the loop between your thumb and forefinger, and turn it to make a three-turn spiral. Bend the wire in an "S" shape, and make a loop on the end to form a hook.
b. String the spiral end of the hook onto the open loop on the prism hanger. Close the prism hanger loop.

⑥ String Beads onto the Fibers
String the remaining 8mm beads onto the fibers, and tie overhand knots to hold them in place.

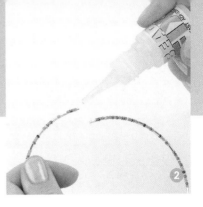

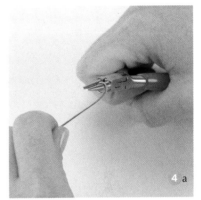

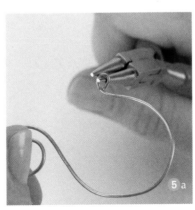

Ribbon and Bead Frame

Materials:

8" square wooden frame

70 grams green/blue/turquoise
  5mm to 8mm glass beads
  in assorted shapes

4 blue 10" lengths
  of 7/8" satin ribbon

4 white 10" lengths of
  26-gauge craft wire

2 oz. white acrylic paint

8 glue dots

Satin acrylic liquid sealer

Adhesive tape

Tools

Sandpaper

1" paintbrush

Wire cutters

Scissors

A basic wooden frame, beads, ribbon and paint are all it takes to create a colorful, inexpensive home accent. Use beaded picture frames to add a handmade touch to any room of the house. Make several frames with coordinating beads to create a collection.

Instructions

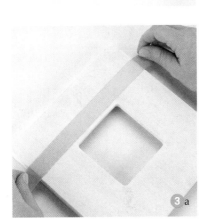

① Prepare the Wood
Follow the instructions on page 29 for preparing unfinished wooden items.

② Paint the Frame
Paint the frame white. Let the paint dry thoroughly between coats. Apply a coat of sealer.

③ Attach the Ribbons
a. Lay a piece of ribbon along one edge of the center cutout.
b. Place a glue dot on the back of each ribbon end, wrap it around to the back of the frame, and attach it.

④ Weave the Ribbons
Use the technique from Step 3 to attach all of the ribbons to the frame. Overlap the ribbons as shown in the photo.

⑤ String Beads onto the Wires
Place a piece of adhesive tape over one end of each piece of wire. String beads for 8". Place a piece of tape over the wire to prevent any beads from sliding off.

⑥ Attach the Wires to the Frame
a. Lay a beaded wire on top of one of the ribbons.
b. Wrap the ends to the back of the frame and twist them together. Cut off any extra wire. Use this technique to attach all of the beaded wires to the frame.

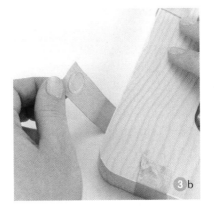

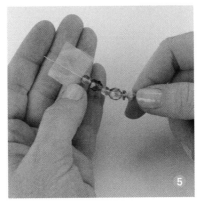

Tip
For an even quicker version of this project, simply embellish a store-bought frame with ribbon and beads.

Embellished Table Setting

Materials for One Place Mat and Napkin Ring Set

19" x 14" turquoise fabric place mat

Coordinating embroidered appliqué for the placemat

30" turquoise/green/ white beaded fringe

3 continuous loops of bracelet-size memory wire

17 green 6mm bicone glass beads

17 turquoise 8mm bicone glass beads

35 green size 6/0 seed beads

35 turquoise size 6/0 seed beads

2 silver 6mm end caps

Turquoise thread

Epoxy or super glue

Fabric glue

Tools

Scissors

Sewing needle

Memory wire shears

Tip

Use beads that coordinate with your dishes, or make all-purpose special-occasion beaded sets with clear crystal beads. Follow the beaded trim and glue packaging instructions for washing directions.

Give your dining table a face-lift with beaded place mats and napkin rings. Choose the beaded trim first, and then purchase coordinating beads for the napkin rings. The napkin ring also doubles as a bracelet!

Instructions for One Place Mat and Napkin Ring Set

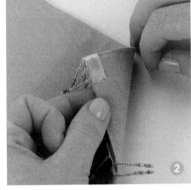

① Attach Beaded Trim

a. Apply a bead of glue along one short edge of the place mat.
b. Fold the end of the beaded trim ribbon, and glue it to the back of the placemat. Working from this end, press the beaded trim ribbon into the glue. Use your fingers to press out any air bubbles.

② Finish the Trim End

Leaving ¼", cut off the rest of the beaded trim. Fold the end under, and glue it to the place mat. Attach the remaining beaded trim to the other side of the place mat.

③ Attach an Embroidered Appliqué

Use fabric glue to attach an embroidered appliqué to the lower right-hand corner of the place mat. Thread a needle, and use it to make a few small stitches to tack down the appliqué.

④ Glue End Caps to the Wire

a. Place a drop of glue on the end of the memory wire, and attach an end cap.
b. Place a turquoise 6/0 bead, green size 6/0 bead and an end cap onto the wire end. Spot-glue the beads and the end cap together. Let the glue dry.

⑤ String Beads

String beads as follows onto the wire: green 6mm bicone, turquoise size 6/0 bead, green size 6/0 bead, turquoise 8mm bicone, green size 6/0 bead and turquoise 6/0 bead.

⑥ Repeat the Beading Pattern

Repeat the beading pattern (from Step 5) 17 times. When you reach the end, look back over the beads to check that the pattern is accurate before proceeding to Step 7.

⑦ Finish the Wire End

Cut the wire end to about ⅛" long. Place a drop of glue on the end of the memory wire. Spot-glue the last few beads and the end cap together. Let the glue dry.

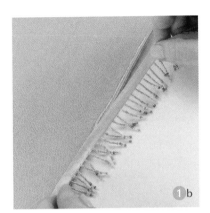

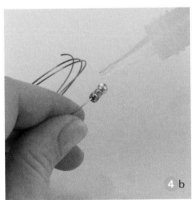

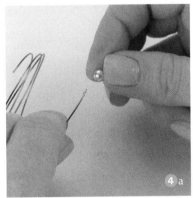

Lacy Candleholder

Materials

4½" contoured glass candleholder

50 peridot 8mm bicone glass beads

3 yd. size .024" (.61mm) flexible beading wire

4 silver 1.3mm crimp beads

Adhesive tape

Tools

Crimping tool

Wire cutters

This simple technique is a modern take on the lacy, open look of macramé—without the knots. I first made a bracelet with this design, and then decided it would be a pretty embellishment for home decor.

Tip
This beaded pattern also would make a great bracelet or choker—just add a clasp to the end.

Instructions

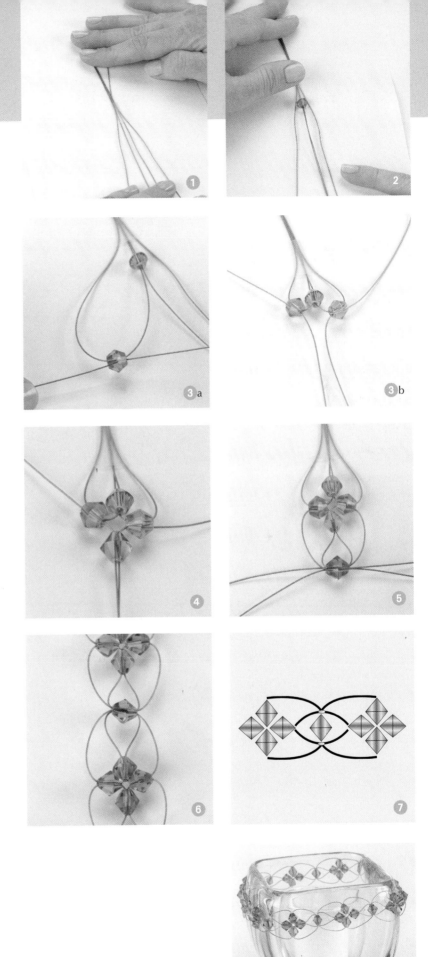

① Prepare the Beading Wire
Cut the beading wire in half. Hold the strands together, and fold them in half. Leave about 3" at the end, and tape the wires to your work surface.

② String the First Bead
Hold the two inner wires together, and string a bead.

③ String the Side Beads
a. String an outer wire and an inner wire through opposite ends of a bead. Pull the wires to adjust the bead so it is perpendicular to the first bead.
b. Repeat this step using the opposite outer and inner wires.

④ Create a Diamond Shape
Hold the inner wires together, and string a bead. Adjust the beads to create a diamond pattern.

⑤ Complete the Beading Pattern
Hold an outer wire and an inner wire together and string them through a bead. Hold the other wires together, and string them through the opposite ends of a bead.

⑥ Repeat the Beading Pattern
Repeat Steps 2 through 5 until the beaded piece is long enough to wrap around the candleholder.

⑦ Attach a Crimp Bead
Remove the adhesive tape from the wire ends. String a crimp bead onto one of the inner wires. String the corresponding wire from the other end of the beadwork through the opposite end of the crimp bead. Adjust the wires so the pattern is maintained. Crimp it. Because the area is so tight, it may be necessary to use chain nose pliers instead of a crimping tool. Use crimp beads to connect all of the wire ends.

Decorative Flowerpot

Materials

5" high terra cotta flowerpot with 16" rim and saucer

8 crystal 2-hole metal slides

8 purple 6mm faceted bicone beads

33 grams purple seed bead mix

19" size .015" (0.38mm) flexible beading wire

2 silver 1.5mm crimp tubes

8 silver head pins

2 oz. acrylic paint: white, purple

Satin acrylic spray sealer

Glue for glass and metal

Tools

Round nose pliers

Chain nose pliers

Wire cutters

1" paintbrush

Clothespins (optional)

Paper towels

Tip

For a quick and easy decorative pot: Paint the flowerpot. Spread a thick layer of waterproof glue onto the rim. Sprinkle seed beads and tiny marbles onto the pot. Let it dry. Apply a coat of liquid acrylic sealer. This version is OK for outdoor pots, too.

I like to purchase starts from local farmer's markets, and I gradually am replacing their utilitarian pots with more decorative pots like this one. This flowerpot is meant for indoor use only.

Instructions

1 Basecoat the Flowerpot

Paint the inside and outside of the pot and saucer white. Let them dry.

2 Paint the Flowerpot

Paint a few strokes of purple paint onto the lower part of the pot, and then use a paper towel to quickly wipe off the purple paint. Use this technique to create a textured look on the lower part of the pot and on the saucer. Let them dry.

3 Seal the Flowerpot

Seal the pot (inside and outside) and saucer with satin acrylic sealer. Let them dry.

4 Attach the Metal Slides

Arrange the crystal/metal slides, evenly spaced, around the rim of the pot. Glue them on the pot when you are satisfied with the placement. If necessary, use clothespins to hold them in place until the glue dries.

5 Attach the Beading Wire

String one end of the beading wire through a hole on the slide. String the other end through the other hole on the same side of the slide. Pull the beading wire so the ends are even.

6 Bead the Flowerpot Rim

String purple seed beads onto both wires to cover the wire between slides. Cross the wires in an "X", and place the ends through the holes on the same side of the slide. Repeat this step seven times to bead the entire pot rim.

7 Crimp the Wire End

Place one wire end back through the first slide. String a crimp bead onto the wire, and pull the wire taut. Use chain nose pliers to crimp it and hold it in place. Repeat for the other wire end. The crimp will prevent the wire end from slipping back through the hole.

8 Cut off Extra Wire

Give the crimped wires a gentle tug to make sure they are securely fastened. Carefully cut off any extra wire.

9 Make Beaded Charms

String each purple 6mm bead onto a head pin. There are eight charms. Use round nose pliers to make a loop above each bead. Cut off any extra wire.

10 Attach Beaded Charms

Use chain nose pliers to open the head pin loops. Connect one head pin loop to each "X" on the flowerpot rim. Close the loops.

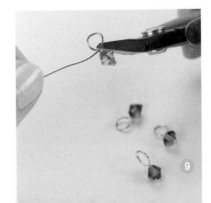
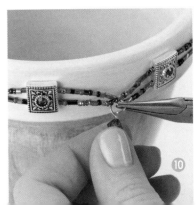

Beads and Baubles Tassel

Materials for One Tassel

Amber 8mm bicone glass bead

Brown 10mm smooth
  round glass bead

Gold/clear 12mm
  smooth round glass bead

8 grams gold size 6/0 seed beads

18 grams brown/gold size 11/0
  seed bead assortment

16 topaz 4mm bicone glass beads

22 brown 4mm round glass beads

8 amber 6mm
  firepolish glass beads

3" gold 18-gauge wire

6" gold 26-gauge wire

1 yd. white size .008"
  (.020mm) beading thread

Antique gold chain bracelet
  with lobster clasp

Jeweler's cement

Tools

Round nose pliers

Chain nose pliers

Wire cutters

Beading scissors

Collapsible eye beading needle

Beaded tassels look complicated, but they're actually very easy to make. Use them to add a decorative touch to curtains, fan pulls, vases and more. I was inspired to make this one because a friend of mine has a little beaded purse hanging from her doorknob—it looks so eclectic and stylish.

Instructions for One Tassel

1 Make an Eye Pin
Use round nose pliers to make a loop on one end of the 3" gold wire. Eye pins made from thinner wire are widely available, but for this project, it is best to make your own from heavier wire.

2 Bead the Eye Pin
String a 12mm bead, 10mm bead and an 8mm bead onto the wire eye pin. Use round nose pliers to make a loop above the top bead. Cut off any extra wire.

3 Bead a Fringe
Thread the needle and tie a double knot 2" from one end of the thread. String seed beads for ¾" to 1", then string assorted seed beads, 4mm and 6mm beads for 1½" to 3". The last bead should be a seed bead.

4 Secure a Fringe
Thread the needle back through the second-to-last bead. Thread it upward through the entire beaded strand. Tie a knot at the top. Repeat Steps 3 and 4 to make 12 fringes.

5 Attach the Tassel
When all of the fringes are complete, thread the ends through opposite sides of the lower loop on the beaded eye pin.

6 Tie the Tassel
Tie the thread ends in a double square knot. Add a drop of glue. Cut off any extra thread.

7 Attach the Wire
Make a loop on one end of the 6" wire piece. Attach the loop to the lower loop on the beaded eye pin.

8 Bead the Wire
String beads to cover the wire, except for the last ¼". Use round nose pliers to bend the end in a loop.

9 Create a Beaded Coil
Wrap the beaded wire around the lower eye pin loop to make a coil. The coil should cover the loop as well as the upper portion of the beaded fringe.

10 Attaching the Chain
Open the upper eye pin loop, and attach it to the center link on the chain.

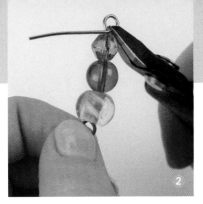
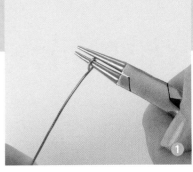

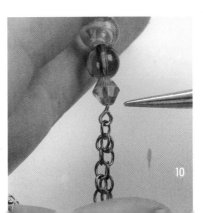

Beaded Towel Rack and Hand Towel

Materials and Tools for the Rack

"Bath" rack with hooks

70 grams blue
  seed bead mix

33 grams clear tiny marbles

2 oz. blue acrylic paint

Dimensional glaze

Craft glue

Sandpaper

1" paintbrush

Old paintbrush

Materials and Tools for the Towel

15½" white hand towel

17½" blue ⅝"
  grosgrain ribbon

10 to 11 blue ⅝" buttons

15½" blue beaded trim

Straight dress pins

Fabric glue

Blue sewing thread

Sewing needle

Scissors

Brighten up your bathroom with a beaded towel rack and decorative hand towel. I used a rack that spells out the word "bath," but you also could use a plain rack with hooks or cut out your own wooden rack that spells another word, like "dream" or "wish."

Instructions for the Rack

1 Prepare the Wood
Prepare the wood, referring to the instructions on page 29.

2 Paint the Rack
Use a 1" paintbrush to paint the bath rack blue.

3 Apply Glue
Use a craft stick or your finger to spread a thick layer of glue onto one of the letters.

4 Attach Beads
Sprinkle seed beads onto the glue, then add tiny marbles. Add glue and beads to the rest of the letters, one letter at a time. Let the glue dry completely.

5 Seal the Beads
Use an old paintbrush to spread dimensional glaze over the beads. Let it dry.

Instructions for the Towel

1 Attach Beaded Trim
Apply a line of fabric glue across the front of the towel. Starting at one side, press the beaded trim into the glue. Cut off any extra trim.

2 Attach Ribbon
Pin the ribbon in place across the top of the beaded trim, leaving at least 1½" extra on each side. Fold the ends under, wrap them to the back of the towel, and pin them in place.

3 Attach Buttons
Knot the thread end. Sew through the ribbon on the back of the towel to attach a button to the front of the towel. Once the button is attached, tie a knot on the back of the towel, and cut the thread. Add buttons evenly spaced on the ribbon.

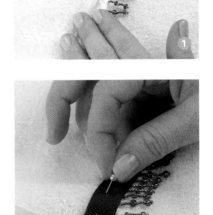

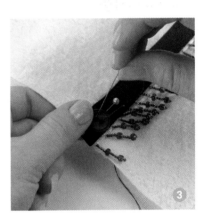

Copper and Patina Keepsake Box

Materials

6⅛" x 6⅛" x 4⅝" wooden
  keepsake box with knob

8 yd. copper-coated
  18-gauge craft wire

25" multicolored
  (green/brown/gold) beaded trim

4¼" square of copper mesh

20″ gold ¾" satin ribbon

2 oz. green acrylic paint

Satin acrylic liquid sealer

Glue for glass and metal

⅛" wide double-sided adhesive tape

Tools

Fine sandpaper

1" bristle paintbrush

Scissors

Craft stick

Round nose pliers

Nylon jaw pliers

Wire cutters

An embellished box keeps keys, change and other daily essentials out of sight but within easy reach on an entry table, nightstand or desk. I like to decorate with boxes because they're the best of both worlds—pretty objects that also are functional.

Instructions

1 Prepare the wood.
Prepare the wood referring to the instructions on page 29.

2 Paint the Box
Paint the box, lid and knob green. Seal all of the pieces.

3 Attach Adhesive Tape
Attach 1/8" double-sided adhesive tape to the rim of the box just
below the lid. Remove the paper backing from the adhesive tape.

4 Attach Beaded Trim
Starting at the back of the box, press the top edge of the beaded trim onto
the double-sided adhesive tape. Overlap the ends. Cut a small piece of
double-sided adhesive, and use it to hold the overlapped end in place.

5 Make Wire Spirals
Cut 18 pieces each of 5" and 7" copper craft wire. Make a loop
on the end of each wire. Grasp the loop inside the nylon jaw
pliers, and turn your wrist to form each wire into a spiral.

6 Attach the Spirals
Use a craft stick to spread a thin layer of glue on the
back of each spiral. Glue nine spirals to each side of the
lid rim, alternating smaller and larger spirals.

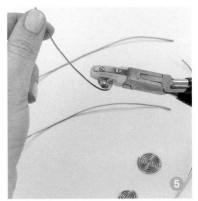

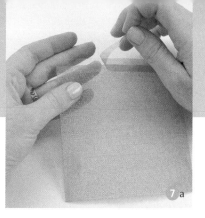

⑦ Cover the Mesh Edges

a. Place ¼" adhesive tape along one edge of the copper mesh.
b. Press the gold ribbon onto the tape with about half of the ribbon overlapping the top edge and about ¼" overlapping each side edge. Place tape on the back of the mesh, and fold the ribbon over to adhere the ribbon to the back of the mesh. Fold the sides in, and use tape to secure them.

⑧ Attach the Mesh to the Box

a. Place tape on the back of the ribbon. Position the copper mesh square on the center of the top of the box as shown. Use a craft knife to cut an "X" in the mesh that covers the knob hole on the top center of the box.
b. Glue the knob into the hole.

⑨ Make Wire Corners

Cut four 16" pieces of copper wire. Fold each one in the center, and spiral the ends.

⑩ Attach Wire Corners to the Box

Glue a wire piece to each corner of the box with the spirals overlapping the ribbon.

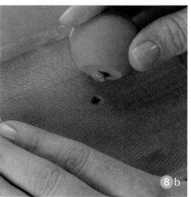

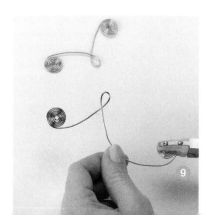

Bejeweled Chandelier

Materials

5-arm chandelier to embellish

135 pink 6mm firepolish beads

20 rose 4mm firepolish beads

10 clear 8mm rondelles

5 clear 8mm teardrops

100 assorted clear and pink 4mm to 8mm firepolish beads

Lengths of gold 24-gauge craft wire: 20 of 12" and 16 of 4"

Lengths of gold 16-gauge craft wire: 5 each; 4" and 18"

5 gold 8½" lengths size .015" (0.38mm) 7-strand flexible beading wire

10 gold 1.3mm crimp beads

5 gold head pins

Tools

Round nose pliers

Chain nose pliers

Wire cutters

Crimping tool

Ruler

A beaded chandelier makes a dramatic centerpiece for a dining room or entryway. I bought an inexpensive chandelier at my local hardware store and embellished it for a fraction of what a store-bought beaded chandelier costs.

Instructions

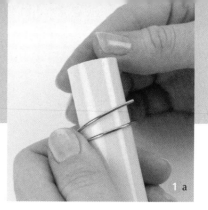

1 a

① Make a Wire Ring

a. Wrap a 4" piece of 16-gauge wire around a candlestick base to form a ring.

b. Use round nose pliers to make a loop on one end.

c. Bend the other end in a 90-degree angle. Place the bent end through the loop to fasten it. Make a wire ring for each candlestick base.

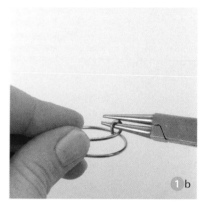

1 b

② Make Beaded Clusters

a. To make a beaded cluster, string a clear or pink 4mm to 8mm firepolish bead onto the center of a 12" wire. Fold the wire so it is doubled. Twist it together for 1½" to 2".

b. String another clear or pink 4mm to 8mm firepolish bead onto one of the wire ends. Position it just below the first bead so that the branch will be slightly shorter. Fold the wire, and twist it together. Repeat for the other end of the wire. Make five beaded clusters for each candlestick base.

1 c

Tip

For a quick and easy version, purchase small lampshades for each candlestick bulb. Glue beaded trim to the lower rim of each shade. Voila! Instant style.

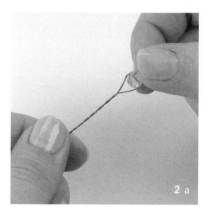

2 a

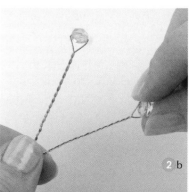

2 b

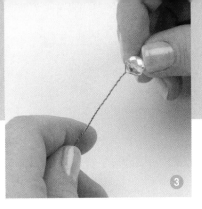

③ Make a Single-Beaded Branch

String a clear or pink 8mm firepolish bead onto the center of a 4" wire. Fold the wire so it is doubled. Twist it together for 1½" to 2". Make five single-beaded branches for each candlestick base.

④ Attach the Clusters

Attach the beaded clusters and single-beaded branches, alternating on the ring by wrapping the wire ends in opposite directions.

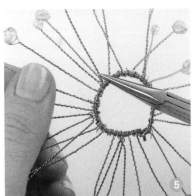

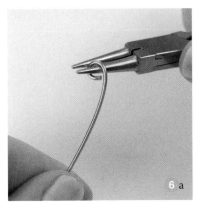

⑤ Finish the Wire Ends

Cut off any extra wire ends, and use chain nose pliers to carefully press the wire ends in. Use your fingers to adjust the beaded clusters.

⑥ Coil the Wire

a. Use round nose pliers to make a loop on one end of an 18" piece of wire.
b. Hold the loop against the top edge of a candlestick base. Wrap the wire downward in a coil around the base. Make a coil for each candlestick base.

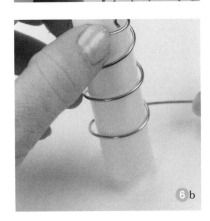

⑦ Make a Teardrop Charm

a. String a teardrop bead onto a head pin.
b. Make a loop above the bead, and attach it to the upper loop on a wire coil. Make five charms, and attach each one to the upper loop on a wire coil.

⑧ Make a Beaded Strand

a. String a crimp bead ½" from the end of a piece of flexible beading wire. Wrap the beading wire around a chandelier arm, and place the end inside the crimp. Crimp it.
b. String beads as follows: nine pink 6mm, one rose 4mm, one rondelle, one rose 4mm, nine pink 6mm, one rose 4mm, one rondelle, one rose

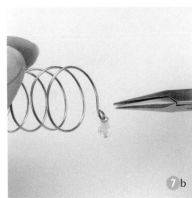

4mm and nine pink 6mm. To attach the other end, string a crimp bead onto the wire. Wrap it around the arm, and place it back inside the crimp. Crimp it. Repeat this step to make a beaded strand for each arm of the chandelier.

Chapter 5: Fashion

A little bit of beading can instantly give an outfit or accessory a designer look. In this chapter, you'll learn how to add simple beading to handbags, clothing, shoes, hats and more. Create your own personal fashion statement!

Chic Beaded Belt

Materials

9 red 10mm firepolish
   glass beads

16 red 10mm rondelle glass beads

17 red 6mm bicone glass beads

31 red size 6/0 seed beads

17 silver 6mm tube beads

16 silver 5mm rondelles

32" size .024" (.61mm)
   49-strand flexible beading wire

10" silver chain

2" silver head pin

31 silver 8mm jump rings

Silver hook crimp clasp

19 silver 1.3mm crimp beads

Tools

Round nose pliers

Chain nose pliers

Crimping tool

Wire cutters

Ruler

I have a funky beaded belt that I wear with a fitted top and my favorite wool skirt. This version is very easy to make and adds a splash of color to a little black dress or a tank top and jeans. It should be worn loosely across the hips. The chain section makes it adjustable from 32" to 42".

Tip

For an even quicker version of this belt, simply make the belt large enough to fit loosely around your hips. Omit the beaded chain, and attach half of the clasp to each end of the belt.

Instructions

1 Attach the Clasp

Place the wire end inside the crimp clasp. Use a crimping tool to close the clasp and secure the wire.

2 Create a Beaded Section

String beads as follows: red bicone, silver tube, red rondelle, silver rondelle, red firepolish, silver rondelle, red rondelle, silver tube and red bicone. String a crimp bead onto the wire, and crimp it to hold the beads in place.

3 Make More Beaded Sections

a. Leave 2" after the beaded unit, and string a crimp bead onto the wire. Crimp it.
b. String another beaded section in the same pattern as in Step 2. String a crimp bead onto the wire, and crimp it to hold the beads in place. Repeat this step until you have a total of eight beaded units.

4 Connect the Wire and Chain

String a crimp bead ½" from the wire end. String one end of the chain onto the wire. Place the wire back inside the crimp bead to form a loop. Crimp it.

5 Attach Beaded Jump Rings

a. String a size 6/0 seed bead onto each jump ring.
b. Attach a beaded jump ring to every other link on the chain.

6 Make a Beaded Charm

a. String a red firepolish, a silver tube and a red bicone bead onto a head pin.
b. Make a loop above the top bead, attach it to the last chain link, and wrap any extra wire around the base of the loop.

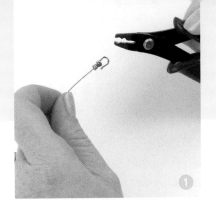

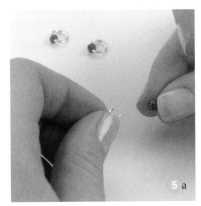

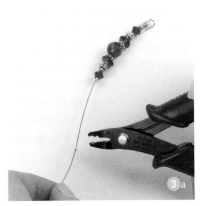

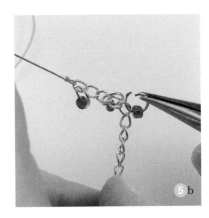

Beaded Sandals

Materials for a Pair of Shoes

Pair of dressy black sandals or shoes

10 metallic 12mm
   tube-shape glass beads

32 metallic 4mm to 8mm
   (assorted shapes) glass beads

2½ yd. black size .008"
   (.20mm) beading thread

Jeweler's cement

Note: *Sample shoes are size nine. Adjust the amount of beads for your shoe size and the amount of straps you plan to embellish.*

Tools

Big eye or collapsible
   eye beading needle

Beading scissors

Use beads to transform a plain pair of sandals to match a special outfit for instant designer pizzazz. Knot the thread, string beads and wrap the thread around the strap. Easy!

Instructions for Each Shoe

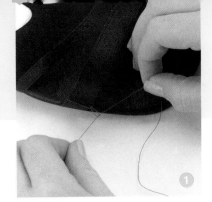

1 Knot the Thread

Wrap the end of the thread around one end of the strap. Tie a knot. Wrap the thread around the strap one more time, and pull it tight to hold it in place. (Red thread is for illustration purposes only.)

2 Wrap the Strap

a. String a tube bead onto the thread. Wrap the thread around the strap two times to hold it in place.
b. String two 4mm to 8mm beads, and repeat the wrapping technique.

3 String Beads

Use the following pattern to create vertical rows across the entire strap: one tube bead, wrap, two 4mm to 8mm beads, wrap, two 4mm to 8mm beads, wrap. Repeat as many times as needed for your shoes.

4 Finish the Strap

Wrap the end of the thread two times around the end of the strap. Tie a knot. Place a drop of jeweler's cement on the knot. Cut off any extra thread.

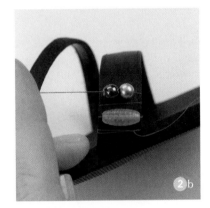

Tip

Use this bead wrapping technique for any strappy shoes, like flip-flops or other casual sandals. For shoes without straps, sew beads directly onto the fabric or soft leather. Use glue for glass and metal to attach rhinestones, cabochons or other flat objects.

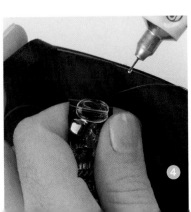

Dramatic Scarf

Materials

20" x 67" cotton
   knit scarf with fringe

2¼ yd. beaded trim to
   coordinate with scarf color

80 size 6/0 glass beads
   (color to match your scarf)

2 yd. size .006" (.15mm)
   beading thread

Fabric glue

Tools

Scissors

Hard beading needle

Needle threader

*A scarf adds instant drama to any outfit. Attach beaded trim
to a long wrap to create this funky, stylish accessory.*

Instructions

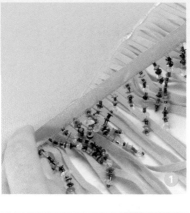

1 **Attach Beaded Trim to the Front**

Apply a line of fabric glue along one end on one side of the scarf. Leave ½" of extra trim on one end and, starting from one edge of the scarf, press the beaded trim into the glue.

2 **Attach Size 6/0 Beads**

Thread the needle, knot the thread end, and stitch a 6/0 bead to the beaded trim ribbon near the long edge of the scarf. Leave ½" and attach another bead to the beaded trim ribbon. Attach a bead every ½" across the beaded trim ribbon. Knot the end on the back of the scarf.

3 **Attach Beaded Trim to the Back**

Turn the scarf over, and glue beaded trim to the other side to cover the beading thread. Overlap the ends, and glue them together.

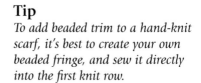

4 **Trim the Fringe**

Cut the fringe so it is about ½" longer than the beaded trim. If your scarf has knotted fringe, remember to re-knot the ends.

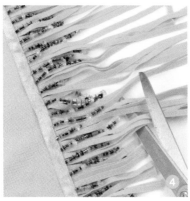

Tip

To add beaded trim to a hand-knit scarf, it's best to create your own beaded fringe, and sew it directly into the first knit row.

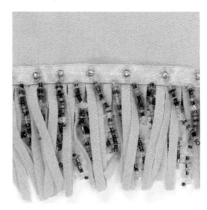

Decorative Checkbook Cover

Materials

Canvas checkbook cover

Geometric rubber stamp

2 tablespoons
  brown/black/gold seed bead mix

7 black ½" buttons

1⅛" x 7⅞" brown leather strip

Black permanent inkpad

1 oz. metallic bronze heat-set paint

Fabric glue

Glue for glass and metal

Dimensional glaze

Tools

Small paintbrush

Paper towel

Iron and ironing board

Craft stick

Who says checkbook covers have to be boring? I made a decorative one so now I can express my creativity with every purchase.

Instructions

1 Stamp the Canvas
Use black ink to stamp the image randomly on the canvas.

2 Paint the Canvas
a. Dip a paintbrush into bronze paint. Tap it onto a paper towel, and then apply light strokes to the canvas between the stamped images.
b. Let the paint dry, then iron the wrong side of the fabric to heat-set the paint.

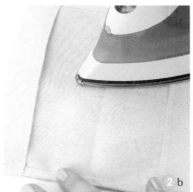

3 Attach the Leather Strip
Apply fabric glue to the back of the leather strip. Glue it across the front of the checkbook cover, about ½" from the lower edge.

4 Attach Buttons
Apply a drop of glue for glass and metal to the back of each button. Glue them evenly spaced across the leather strip.

5 Attach Beads
Use a craft stick to apply a line of craft glue along one long edge of the leather strip, letting the glue overlap the edge. Sprinkle beads onto the glue. Repeat for the other edge of the leather.

6 Seal the Beads
Apply dimensional glaze sparingly over the beads.

Tip
Blank checkbook covers make great canvases for the imagination, because they're fairly small and inexpensive. Use them to experiment with new beading, stamping and painting techniques without worrying about mistakes.

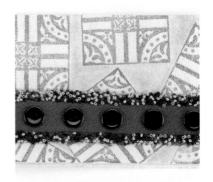

Daisy Chain Cardigan

Materials

Pink cardigan

8 pink 6mm round cat's eye beads

60 pink 4mm round cat's eye beads

56 gray 4mm round glass beads

2 yd. gray size .006"
  (.15mm) beading thread

Note: *A size medium cardigan was used as our sample. You may have to adjust the amount of beads accordingly.*

Tools

Beading scissors

Hard beading needle

Needle threader

This project combines two of my favorite things—cardigans (my wardrobe staple) and daisies. The daisies actually are very easy to make, and they turn an ordinary cardigan into a trendy original.

Instructions

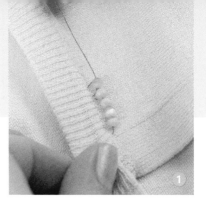

❶ Embroider a Beaded Chain

Thread the needle, and knot the thread end. Stitch from the inside of the sweater close to the neck seam. Thread five pink 4mm beads, and stitch back through the last bead to attach the chain to the sweater.

❷ Make a Daisy

a. String seven gray beads onto the thread. Stitch through the first gray bead to form a circle.
b. String a pink 6mm bead onto the thread, and place the needle back through the fourth bead.
c. Tack the daisy to the sweater by backstitching through each gray bead.

❸ Add Another Chain and Daisy

String five pink 4mm beads onto the thread. Backstitch through the last bead. Follow Step 2 to make another daisy. Repeat Steps 2 and 3 to create three daisies on each side of the sweater.

❹ Add Daisies to the Cuffs

Make a cluster of three daisies near the end of the sleeve.

Tip

Use this simple bead embroidery technique to add daisy chains to pillows, blankets, purses, gloves and more.

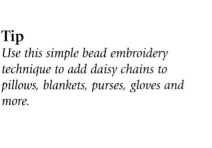

Jazzy Winter Gloves

Materials

Pair of off-white stretchy
   knit gloves with 1¼" cuffs

26 blue 6mm to 8mm
   oval cat's eye beads

36 aqua 6mm firepolish
   glass beads

1½ yd. white size .028"
   (.70mm) stretchy thread

Tools

Big eye needle

Beading scissors

*When there's a long, cold winter ahead, it can be easy to forget about fashion
and just try to stay warm. These easy beaded gloves are the best of both worlds,
because they're cute and comfortable. You might want winter to last a little longer.*

Instructions for One Glove

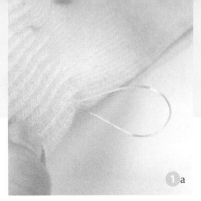

① Knot the Thread
a. Thread the needle. Place the needle through the cuff from the inside, leaving a 2" tail.
b. Place the end back through the cuff, and tie the ends in a knot.

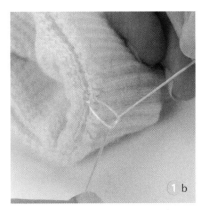

② String the First Row
String beads as follows: two aqua, one cat's eye, and two aqua. Keep the beads in a straight line so they lay between the knitted rows.

③ Make the First Stitch
Press the needle through the cuff, bring it sideways about ¼", and bring it back through to the front of the cuff.

④ String the Second Row
String beads as follows: one cat's eye, two aqua and one cat's eye. Keep the beads in a straight line so that they lay between the knitted rows. Repeat Step 3.

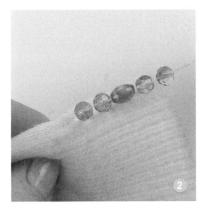

⑤ Finish the Cuff
Repeat the beading pattern from Steps 2 through 4 to add nine beaded rows to the cuff. To tie off the thread, stitch back through the last bead, and knot the thread inside the cuff.

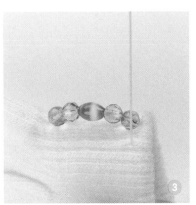

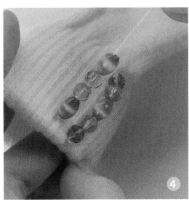

Tip
The beading in this project is meant to stretch when the cuff stretches. If your gloves are not stretchy, you can use regular beading thread. These gloves would make great stocking stuffers!

One-of-a-Kind Denim Jacket

Materials

Denim jacket

24" black/jewel tone beaded trim

2 yd. black size .008"
 (.20mm) beading thread

Fabric glue

Note: The length of the beaded trim depends on the size of your jacket. Our sample was made using size large.

Tools

Beading scissors

Beading needle

Straight dress pins

Scrap cardboard

Make a statement with your own decorated denim jacket. Go casual with a t-shirt and khaki pants or feminine with a camisole and flirty skirt.

Instructions

① Prepare the Pockets

Place a piece of cardboard over the jacket, above the pockets. Fold each pocket flap up, and pin it to the cardboard so the inside of the flap is exposed and held in place.

② Attach Beaded Trim to the Pockets

Apply fabric glue along the edge of one pocket flap. Starting at one side of the flap, press beaded trim into the glue. Cut off the extra trim, and use it for the other pocket.

③ Attach Beaded Trim to the Cuffs

Fold the cuffs back so the inside is exposed. Apply fabric glue along the edge of one cuff. Starting at one side of the cuff, press beaded trim into the glue. Cut off the extra trim, and use it for the other cuff. Let the glue dry.

④ Tack the Beaded Trim

Fold the cuffs down. Thread a needle, and tie a knot in the thread end. Place the needle through the cuff from the inside, near the end of one beaded strand. Stitch over the beaded strand and back into the cuff.

⑤ Finish the Cuffs

Use the technique from Step 4 to tack the beaded strand to each cuff. Knot the thread end and cut off any extra thread.

Tip

Washing Instructions
Follow the washing instructions on the glue bottle and beaded trim packaging. Most beaded items should be washed by hand.

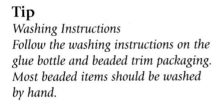

Wire and Bead Headband

Materials

Silver wire headband

36 gray 6mm cat's eye beads

70 matte gray size 6/0 beads

1½ yd. silver 26-gauge craft wire

Tools

Chain nose pliers

Wire cutters

Embellish a store-bought headband with this easy wire and bead technique. They're so quick to make that you could create several in one sitting—keep one for yourself and give others to your firends.

Instructions

① Attach the Wire
Wrap one wire end around the headband near the first wire tooth. Make sure the wire is wrapped in the same direction as the wire between the teeth.

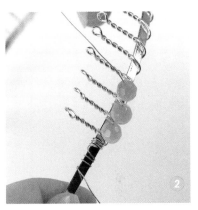

② String a Cat's Eye Bead
String a cat's eye bead onto the 26-gauge wire. Wrap the wire around the headband, positioning the bead between two teeth. Repeat for each cat's eye bead.

③ String All the Cat's Eye Beads
Continue adding beads, wrapping the wire around the headband between each bead until you reach the last tooth. Wrap the wire two to three times around the headband after the last tooth.

④ String Size 6/0 Beads
Wrap the wire diagonally back around the headband between the last two cat's eye beads. String two size 6/0 beads onto the wire. Position one on each side of the headband, and pull the wire tight to hold it in place.

⑤ Finish the Headband
Continue stringing two size 6/0 beads between each cat's eye beads. Wrap the wire two to three times around the headband after the last tooth. Cut off any extra wire.

Tip
Other quick and easy headband ideas:
- *Use glue for glass and metal to attach beads to a plastic headband.*
- *String beads onto beading wire, and connect the ends with a piece of stretchy beading cord.*
- *Use simple stitches to attach beads to a fabric headband.*
- *Try this fun project for a girl's birthday party.*

Dress Up Your Purse

Materials

9" x 5½" black purse with removable strap

16" beaded trim of your choice

15 chunky 15mm Amazonite beads

8 black 8mm round glass beads

8 red 8mm firepolish glass beads

16 gold size 6/0 seed beads

19" size .024" (.61mm) flexible beading wire

2 silver 1.5mm crimp tubes

2 large silver lobster clasps

Fabric glue

Tools

Crimping tool

Wire cutters

It's easy to dress up a basic handbag with a new beaded strap and some pretty beaded trim. Give an old purse a new lease on life, or start from scratch with a new purse. Choose the beaded trim first, then purchase coordinating beads for the strap.

Instructions

① Attach the Beaded Trim

Remove the original strap from the purse. Place a line of glue along the upper edge of the purse. Starting at one edge, press the beaded trim into the glue. Overlap the ends of the beaded trim, and secure them with a drop of glue. Let the glue dry.

② Make a New Strap

a. String a crimp tube ½" from the end of the flexible beading wire. String a clasp onto the wire.
b. Place the wire end back inside the crimp tube to form a loop.

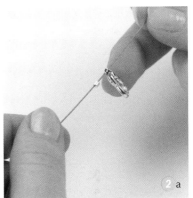

③ Crimp the Strap

Place the crimp tube in the inner jaws of the crimping tool, and squeeze it hard to make an indentation. Remove the crimp tube, turn it 90 degrees, and place it in the outer jaws. Squeeze it gently to fold the crimp in half. See the illustration on page 26.

④ String Beads onto the Strap

String beads as follows onto the strap: gold, black, gold, Amazonite, gold, red and gold. Repeat this pattern to string all the beads.

⑤ Finish the Strap

String a crimp tube and lobster clasp onto the wire. Place the wire end back inside the crimp tube to form a loop. Adjust the strap so there is a little space between the last bead and the crimp tube. This will ensure that the strap stays flexible. Crimp it, and cut off any extra wire. Open each lobster clasp, and attach each to the strap attachment inside the purse.

Tip

For an all-purpose beaded purse, omit the beaded trim. Create several straps in different styles and change them to match your outfits.

Cigar Box Purse

Materials

6½" x 7¼" unfinished
   wooden cigar box

10 dark brown 12mm
   round wooden beads

20 light brown 10mm
   round wooden beads

11 gold plastic pony beads

3" x 4" brown doeskin leather

3½" oval picture
   frame rubber stamp

1 set of 3-D alphabet
   stickers to spell "WISH"

5¼" gold 3/4" satin ribbon

2 oz. brown acrylic paint

Brass handle with removable ends

2 brass brackets with screws

4 brass corners

Black permanent inkpad

Satin acrylic sealer

Craft glue

Glue for glass and metal

Tools

Sandpaper

1" paintbrush

Scissors

Toothpick

Screwdriver

Tip

*Experiment with other bead styles
to completely change the look of this
purse. Make sure the bead holes are
large enough to fit on the handle.*

*Now that cigar box purse supplies are widely available, you can make
your own personalized handbag for a fraction of the boutique price. Paint
and decorate the box, then add a beaded handle for instant style.*

Instructions

① Prepare the Wood
Prepare the wood referring to the instructions on page 29.

② Paint the Box
Wet your paintbrush and dip it into brown paint. Apply a light wash to the entire box.

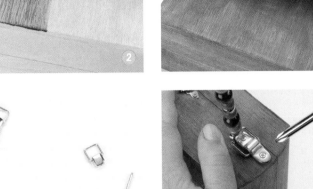

③ Antique the Box
Lightly sand the wooden box again. Scuff the edges to create an aged, vintage look. Apply another coat of acrylic sealer. Let it dry.

④ Bead the Handle
Remove one end of the brass handle. String beads as follows: gold bead, light brown bead, dark brown bead and light brown bead. Repeat this beading pattern to cover the rest of the handle with beads. String another gold bead, and attach the end of the handle.

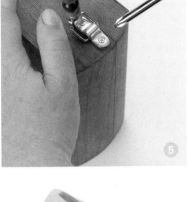

⑤ Attach the Handle
Hold one bracket in place along the opening edge of the box. Place the end of a handle under the bracket. Place a screw in one bracket hole, and screw it in. Attach the other screw. Use the same technique to attach the other bracket.

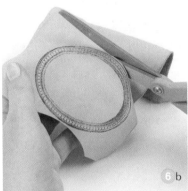

⑥ Make the Medallion
a. Stamp a black picture frame image onto the leather.
b. Cut it out.
c. Fold the ribbon in half and cut the tails in a "V" shape.
d. Glue the fold to the lower edge on the back of the stamped image.
e. Glue the medallion to the box. Add the stickers.

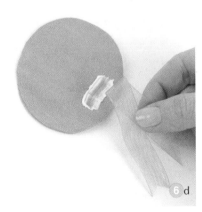

⑦ Add Gold Cord
Use a toothpick to make a thin line of glue along the edge of the stamped leather. Press the gold cord into the glue.

⑧ Attach Brass Corners
Glue a brass corner to each corner on the front of the box.

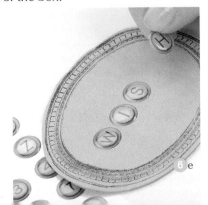

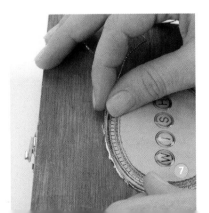

Straw Hat

Materials

Straw hat with 25" crown (circumference)

30 aqua 8mm firepolish glass beads

150 blue 6mm firepolish glass beads

15 blue 4mm round glass beads

Lengths of 20" size .015" (0.38mm) flexible beading wire: 2

4 silver 1.3mm crimp beads

Tools

Crimping tool

Wire cutters

Adhesive tape

Even if you're not going to the beach, a straw hat is a smart, stylish look for summertime. A beaded band lends an artistic touch.

Instructions

❶ String the First Bead
Use a piece of tape to attach the wires to a work surface. This will help keep them in place while you work. String a 6mm bead onto one wire. Place the other wire through the opposite end of the bead. Adjust the bead so it is vertical.

❷ Complete the First Stitch
String the following beads onto each wire: 4mm, 8mm and 4mm. Place the wires through opposite ends of a 6mm bead. Adjust the beads to form a circle.

❸ Make the Second Stitch
String a 6mm bead onto each wire, and then place the wires through opposite ends of another 6mm bead. Adjust the beads to form a diamond shape.

❹ Complete the Beading Pattern
Make two more stitches using 6mm beads.

❺ Bead the Band
Repeat Steps 2 through 4 until the beaded band is long enough to fit around the hat.

❻ Finish the Band
To connect the last stitch to the first stitch, remove the tape, and string a crimp bead onto each wire end. Place the wires through opposite ends of the first bead, stringing them through the crimp beads in an "X". Crimp them.

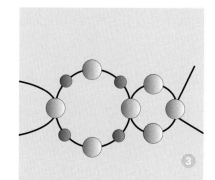

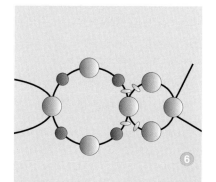

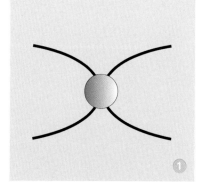

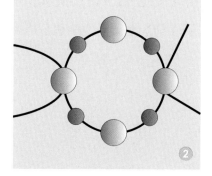

Charm Bracelet Purse

Materials for the Beaded Strap

84 clear 8mm round faceted glass beads

4 mauve 8mm round faceted glass beads

3 aqua 8mm round faceted glass beads

3 blue 8mm round faceted glass beads

3 yellow 8mm round faceted glass beads

26 silver 8mm bead caps

1 yd. size .024" (.61mm) flexible beading wire

2 silver 1.5mm crimp tubes

Satin purse with strap attachments

Tools for the Beaded Strap

Crimping pliers

Wire nippers

Materials for the Charm Bracelet

Silver charm bracelet; blank without clasp

Silver charms: "imagine," "nurture," "inspire," "trust," and "live" (You may substitute for charms of your choice)

2 each; blue, clear, mauve, yellow, aqua, amethyst round 8mm faceted glass beads

2 each; green, lavender 6mm round faceted glass beads

4 silver 8mm bead caps

4 silver 5mm spacer beads

16 silver head pins

This project combines two popular accessories—handbags and bracelets. A girl never can have too many of either one! The bracelet is used to embellish the purse, but it also can be worn separately.

2 silver toggle clasps

5 silver 6mm split rings

2 silver 8mm jump rings

6 silver 6mm jump rings

Tools for the Charm Bracelet

Round nose pliers

Chain nose pliers

Wire nippers

Split ring pliers

Instructions for the Beaded Strap

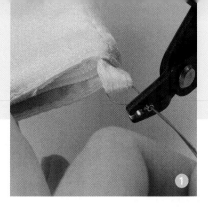

1 Attach One End of the Strap

String a crimp tube onto the beading wire, and place one end of the beading wire through the strap attachment. Place the wire end back into the crimp tube to form a loop. Leave a 1" tail. Use crimping pliers to squeeze the crimp tube.

2 Add Another Crimp Tube

a. String a clear bead and another crimp tube onto the beading wire.
b. Thread the 1" tail through the bead and crimp tube. Crimp the tube. The finished strap will be fairly heavy, so adding the second crimp tube will make the strap stronger. String five more clear beads.

3 String Beads onto the Strap

String a bead cap, a colored bead, a bead cap and six clear beads onto the strap. Repeat this beading pattern 12 times.

4 Attach the Other End of the Strap

String five clear beads, a crimp tube, a clear bead and a crimp tube. Place the beading wire end through the strap attachment and back into the crimp tube to form a loop. Thread the tail through the last few beads and extra crimp tube. Adjust the beads so the strap is flexible. If the beading wire is too tight, the strap will be stiff. Crimp the crimp tubes.

Tip
Use birthstone-colored beads and kid-themed charms to make a mother's bracelet.

Instructions for the Charm Bracelet

① Attach Silver Charms to the Bracelet Blank
a. Attach a split ring to each silver charm using split ring pliers.
b. Attach the charms, spaced evenly on the bracelet blank. Leave five blank links between each charm.

② Make the Beaded Charms
String a clear 8mm bead onto a head pin. Use round nose pliers to make a loop above the bead. Cut off any excess wire. Repeat this technique to make a single-bead charm with the other clear bead, the yellow beads and the lavender and green 6mm beads. Make a double-bead charm using a blue bead and a bead cap; repeat. Make a double-bead charm using an amethyst bead and a silver spacer bead; repeat. Make a beaded charm using an aqua bead and a metal spacer bead; repeat.

③ Attach Beaded Charms to the Bracelet Blank
a. Use chain nose pliers to open the loops on two single-bead charms. Open the loops to the side, rather than pulling the ends directly away from each other. Attach both of the single-bead charms to the center bracelet link between two silver charms.
b. Attach one double-bead charm to a bracelet link on each side of the single-bead charms. Repeat this pattern to attach all of the beaded charms to the bracelet blank.

④ Attach the Clasp to the Bracelet
Use a 6mm jump ring to attach half of the toggle clasp to each end of the bracelet.

⑤ Attach the Other Clasp to the Purse
Connect two 6mm jump rings to each other, and attach the straight part of the unused toggle clasp to one ring. Connect an 8mm jump ring to the other end and attach it to the strap attachment. Connect two more split rings to each other, and attach the round part of the toggle clasp to one ring. Connect a jump ring to the other end, and attach it to the strap attachment.

⑥ Fasten the Bracelet onto the Purse
Attach each bracelet clasp end to the corresponding clasp on the purse.

Resource Guide

The projects in this book are made from materials that are widely available. The following companies generously provided sample products.

Beading Supplies

Beadalon®*
(866) 4-BEADALON
www.beadalon.com
Beadalon® flexible beading wires
Remembrance™ memory wire
Elasticity™ stretchy cord
ColourCraft® wire
Dandyline™ beading thread
Cat's eye and glass beads
Beading tools
Bead Fix™ glue
GS Hypo Cement™ jeweler's cement
Organizers
Stackable containers
Wooden organizer

The Beadery®*
(800) 422-4472
www.thebeadery.com
Elements™ pink plastic bead mix

Blue Moon Beads*
(800) 377-6715
www.bluemoonbeads.com
Glass beads
Metal charms and findings

Halcraft USA, Inc.*
(212) 376-1580
www.halcraft.com
Tiny marbles
Bead Heaven glass beads
Satin picture frames

Pure Allure
pajewelry@aol.com
Crystal Innovations™
Swarovski® crystal beads

Thunderbird Supply Company
(800) 545-7968
www.thunderbirdsupply.com
Silver "Believe" bead
Chunky Amazonite beads

General Supplies

All Night Media, Inc.®
(800) 842-4197
www.allnightmedia.com
Anna Griffin™ oval picture
frame rubber stamp

API Crafter's Pick™*
(510) 526-7616
www.crafterspick.com
The Ultimate! craft glue

Bagworks™*
(800) 365-7423
www.bagworks.com
Canvas pillow cover
Additions™ white satin purse
Additions™ black baguette purse
Canvas checkbook cover

Beacon Adhesives™*
(914) 699-3400
www.beacon1.com
Glass, Metal and More glue
Fabri-Tac™ permanent adhesive

Generations®*
(314) 542-5400
www.generationsnow.com
Sassy Scrapper™ photo organizer

Darice®*
(800) 321-1494
www.darice.com
Unfinished cigar box and hardware
Bead organizer tins

Hampton Art*
(800) 229-1019
www.hamptonart.com
Paris moments Diffusion™
rubber stamp 4557 Jill Meyer
Circle crest Diffusion™ rubber
stamp 4450 Walter Knabe
Pocket watch Diffusion™ rubber
stamp 2167 Diana Kovacs
Passport Diffusion™ rubber
stamp 4521 Jill Meyer

Hansen Brand Source
(800) 773-4746
990 W. Fulton Street
Waupaca, WI 54981
www.homeappliances.com/hansen
Photo shoot location

Hirschberg-Schutz and Co., Inc.*
(908) 810-1111
Decorative Details™ beaded
trim and embroidered ribbon
Style-a-bility beaded trim
Charming Thoughts silver/
pink crown charm

Hot Off The Press®
(800) 227-9595
www.craftpizazz.com
Paper Pizazz™ patterned papers
and grape jelly fibers

Jacquard Products®*
(800) 442-0455
www.jacquardproducts.com
Pearl Ex metallic stamp pads
Lumiere™ metallic paints

Judikins*
(310) 515-1115
www.judikins.com
Diamond Glaze™
dimensional adhesive

Loew-Cornell®*
(201) 836-7070
www.loew-cornell.com
American Painter® 4450 1" paintbrush

Midwest Products Co., Inc.*
(800) 348-3497
www.midwestproducts.com
½" x 12" x 12" craft plywood

Postmodern Design
(405) 321-3176
postmoderndesign@aol.com
English Tile Cube rubber
stamp HD1-101-G

Provo Craft®*
(800) 937-7686
www.provocraft.com
Art Accentz™ Treasure Beadz, Micro
Beadz and Microfine Sparklerz
Art Accentz™ Terrifically Tacky Tape
8" wooden picture frame

Stampabilities®
(800) 888-0321
www.craftsetc.com
Rosetta window rubber stamp F1085

Tidy Craft
(208) 523-2565
www.tidycrafts.com
Eclipse bead organizer

Tsukineko®*
(800) 769-6633
www.tsukineko.com
Brilliance metallic inkpads
Black Stayz-On® permanent inkpad

Walnut Hollow®*
(800) 395-5995
www.walnuthollow.com
5319 unfinished wooden
carriage clock
1112 clock face
TQ600P clock movement
25437 unfinished wooden rack
3209 unfinished wooden box

Westrim®*
(800) 727-2727
www.westrimcrafts.com
Linen-covered scrapbook

These are distributor and wholesale companies only. Check their Web sites for retail listings, and ask for these products at your local craft store.